The FATHER REVEALED

G. Craig Lauterbach

ISBN 1-58169-112-2
For Worldwide Distribution
Printed in the U.S.A.

Evergreen Press
P.O. Box 191540 • Mobile, AL 36619
800-367-8203

TABLE OF CONTENTS

DEDICATION

I am dedicating this book to my loving and faithful
heavenly Father who has blessed me beyond the expression
of words. Without Him there would be no book, without
Him I would have no life at all. He truly is the
Father I always longed for!

I love you!

ACKNOWLEDGMENTS

I would like to thank the following individuals
for their support in helping to bring God's vision for this
book to pass. Without your prayers, faith, confidence, en-
couragement, and support this would have never become a
reality. Like Aaron and Hur, the servants of Moses, you have
held up my arms so the Father could reveal
Himself to a lost and hurting world.

Christopher Dewey, Russ & Suze Thorne, Lloyd
Hildebrand, Keith Carroll, Pastor Tommy Barnett, Robert
Stearns, Pastor John and Carol Arnott, Robert Strand,
Reverend Stewart Deal, Dr. David Yonggi Cho, Brian &
Kathy Banashak, Evergreen Press, all of my C.L.M. sup-
porters, Patience Akuoko, Stephanie Venettone, my Mom
and especially my wife Cindy and four daughters
Kelley, Heather, Heidi, and Laura.

THANK YOU!

FOREWORD

In *The Father Revealed,* Craig Lauterbach brings us a fresh, vital word that will transform our relationship with God the Father. Today's world, filled with such a multitude of fatherless families, has lost its ability to understand the kind of father/child relationship that God has always desired to have with us. Lauterbach blows the dust from centuries of relegating the Father to stories from the Old Testament and instead, offers us the opportunity to draw closer to Him today and find our lives will never be the same again.

Craig Lauterbach brings God the Father's role into the forefront of our lives. He deftly provides us with an accurate portrait of the Father who loves us so magnificently. Through Scripture and his own life experiences, Lauterbach takes us on a journey to discover how to live in the Father's presence. It is only there that our lives can be eternally transformed.

The power of *The Father Revealed* lies in the complete honesty and vulnerability of Craig Lauterbach and in his ability to accurately hear a vital word from the Father's heart. You will soon find yourself drawn into seeking an intimacy with God the Father that you may never have thought possible. This message has the potential of changing the entire focus of the church, and as a result, transforming the lives of its members.

— *Robert Stearns*
Exec. Director, Eagles' Wings, New York

INTRODUCTION

This book combines the story of how I came to experience and know God as an intimate loving Father with the unfolding truths His Spirit has revealed to me as a result of this newfound relationship.

Prior to this life changing experience, I was what many would call "successful." My church was prospering and my personal ministry was growing, but at the same time there was an emptiness within me that no human being, recreational activity, or social involvement could fill. At that time I didn't realize it, but the root of my struggle was I needed to be made whole. I was experiencing a portion of God's blessing rather than His fullness because my focus was on a portion of God, rather than fullness of His personhood.

In order to enjoy the fullness of God's presence, He must be honored fully, which means knowing Him as Father, Son, and Holy Spirit. My view of God was only two dimensional, focusing on Jesus and the Holy Spirit. Whenever God the Father was mentioned, I struggled to comprehend relationship with Him. I had experienced Jesus at salvation, I had experienced the Holy Spirit's baptism shortly after my conversion, but I had never experienced an encounter with the Father. Without this, I was a crippled Christian. Now, think about that for a moment. Doesn't this currently describe the church at large? Because we lack this revelation of God the Father, we are functioning at a much slower pace of ministry and in some cases, a total impendent state, thus unable to even perform what was considered by the early church as routine. This ought not be!

My prayer is that through this book, the Holy Spirit would impact you as He did my life when I encountered the Father's glory for the first time. I challenge you to get ready for a radical change. Business as usual for your life is over. In fact, business as usual for the church is coming to an end. God is about to show up and introduce Himself.

G. Craig Lauterbach C.L.M.
Pipersville, New Jersey

CHAPTER ONE

Understanding the Father

Philip said to Him, "Lord, show us the Father, and it is sufficient for us" (John 14:8).

The entire earthly ministry of Jesus centered around one thing—doing the will of the Father. His disciples were challenged by this kind of thinking because the concept of God as a Father took them beyond the realm of their traditional Jewish upbringing. Jesus' constant reference to God as Father gave rise to many of their questions, causing Philip to ask Jesus in John 14:8, "Lord, show us the Father, and it will suffice us."

A Father/child relationship is the kind of relationship God has *always* desired to have with mankind. Through His teachings, His fulfillment of prophecy, and His obedience to the Law, Jesus revealed the Father's heart to His disciples. And so, Jesus responded to Philip's plea by saying,

Have I been with you so long, and yet you have not known Me, Philip? He who has seen Me has seen the Father. So how can you say, "Show us the Father" (John 14:9).

Jesus was sent to reveal the Father's heart to us and, though His death on the cross, to restore the relationship between God and man that had been lost because of Adam's disobedience.

Fathers in Today's World

Today many of us have a hard time understanding a true, godly relationship between father and child, which, in turn, affects how we view our heavenly Father. In my own case and like those of the majority of my peers, my father was a wonderful, hard-working man, but one who, unfortunately, didn't realize the importance of our relationship.

My father started his own cleaning business as a young man, providing janitorial service for businesses such as hospitals, office buildings, and airports. We lived in the thriving Baltimore/Washington area, so the demand for this type of service was constantly increasing. His company quickly prospered and brought abundant financial blessings to our family.

Those financial blessings, however, did not come easily. The business required every family member to give 100%, or so it seemed, to the growing company. It often felt as though we worked 24 hours a day, seven days a week. For example, when employees didn't show up for work, we had to work in their place. Although we enjoyed the benefits of the business, we had to pay a steep price in order to do so. Many times we had to cancel dates and miss special engagements and church events in order to fulfill the demands of a family-owned business. My father's professional obligations *always* took precedence over everything else.

I remember one incident in particular that deeply affected me. I was nine years old, and school had just recessed for the summer. The men's ministry of our local church was getting ready to sponsor their annual father-and-son softball game. I was excited to think that my father and I would be able to play in the game together! I ran home with the registration form to fill out with my dad. When he handed me back the completed form, he solemnly promised to show up for the game. I was absolutely elated and eagerly began to count down the remaining days until the anticipated game.

On the afternoon of the event, I was at the ballfield 30 minutes in advance and kept a constant eye out for my father's arrival. This was the most exciting day of my life. However, by the 2:00 game time, Dad had not yet shown up. Were there were some last-minute details he had to tend to? Where was he? I knew he just had to come because he had given me his word.

The game began but still no dad! My first time up at bat I looked to see if he was watching, but my father was nowhere to be found. As the realization began to dawn on me that he might not come at all, I felt totally heartbroken. All I wanted to do was go home and hide. Tears welled up from deep within. I felt disappointed, unimportant, abandoned, and unloved.

Later on, when my father finally came home, he apologized, "Sorry, son, I was busy with work, and I simply forgot. I'll make it up to you next time." In a way, the apology almost made it worse because it was obvious that Dad did not understand how important his promise to me had been.

I never played in another father-and-son softball game, not because the games were canceled, but because Dad was always too busy with work. Unbeknownst to him, my father was teaching me that work was more important than anything else. Thus began my journey of always trying to earn my father's attention and love, which would eventually spill over into my relationship with my heavenly Father.

From a job as a teenager to my first pastoral position, this same striving for approval was ingrained into my life and ministry. The truth is that I enjoyed working hard, and when the responsibility of ministry was combined with diligent effort and hard work, I was in my element. Without realizing it at the time, I had embraced a mind-set that easily leads us to operate in our own wisdom and strength rather than flowing out of a relationship with the Father by tapping into His wisdom and strength.

After becoming an assistant pastor of a large church located in New Jersey, this same mentality carried over into my ministry with the youth. I wanted so desperately to have the area's largest and most effective youth outreach. In an effort to fulfill this dream, I planned, trained, and scheduled tremendous amounts of ministry and outreach. But eventually with over 100 teenagers in the youth department, I began to feel very tired and irritable. Little did I realize that my strong ambitions had put me on the verge of burn-out.

By My Spirit

I will never forget the night when God began to speak to me about it. Terry Talbot, a Christian musician and good friend of mine, had come to my church to perform a Friday evening concert. His band had finished setting up and were returning to their hotel to shower, dress, and have dinner. As they left, I told them I'd catch up with them later.

After securing the building, I noticed a casually dressed,

white-haired gentleman standing in the sanctuary and staring at me. I walked over to him and asked if I could be of any help.

He handed me a small piece of white notepaper with writing penciled on it and said, "Young man, read this to me."

I looked at the paper and read aloud,

Not by might, nor by power, but by My Spirit, says the Lord of hosts.

After reading this message, I was amazed because the Holy Spirit had been speaking this very scripture to me through the song, "By My Spirit," which had been resounding in my head all week. In fact, earlier in the day while the band was setting up, the verse had been running over and over again in my head so much so that I had finally turned in my Bible concordance in order to locate the reference for it.

So when the man next asked me, "Where is this verse found?" I was able to quickly respond, "Zechariah 4:6."

He looked straight into my eyes and with an authoritative voice said, "Whenever we utilize God's Word, it's important to know the verse and the reference."

I had never encountered anyone like him before. *Who is this man? How did he know what I had been thinking? Could he be an angel in disguise?*

My mind went back to my grandmother telling me about a white-haired gentleman who came to her home in Baltimore City once a year on the same date for five consecutive years. She never learned his name and only saw him those five times. He always knocked politely on the screen door and asked for a glass of milk and a sandwich.

Each time after she gave him what he asked for, he would scrub the front steps of her row house in response to her hospitality. After the fifth year, she never saw him again. I remember asking her, "Gramma, why did you trust a stranger like that?"

Her reply was a verse from the Bible,

> *Do not neglect to show hospitality to strangers, for by this some have entertained angels without knowing it* (Heb. 13:2 NASB).

I couldn't help but wonder if this was a similar occurrence. While driving to the restaurant to meet Terry and the band members, I found myself wondering again and again, *Could he be an angel?* My excitement surrounding this possibility began to mount. When I returned to the church and opened the doors for the concert, the old gentleman was one of the first ones who entered. He took a seat in the front pew on the inside aisle. As the service proceeded, I was inspired by the way he worshiped.

When the band paused halfway through the concert to collect an offering, I looked over and saw that the white-haired man was gone. It was as if he had vanished right in the middle of the service. Once again I wondered, *Was he an angel?* Whether he was an angel or not, one thing was certain, he was a messenger from God who had been sent to confirm the Holy Spirit's word to me—a word that would eventually become the very foundation of my life and ministry. Human resources and strength will never fully accomplish God's work; it's only by the power of His Spirit that we are able to complete the tasks the Father has given us to do. The seeds of this truth were now planted deep within my heart through this white-haired messenger I've since come to call "The Zechariah Man," but little did I know the road which needed to be walked before this truth would become a reality in my life.

"Never Forget"

Two years later, the Christian music duo "Lamb" was preparing for an evening concert at the same church. While overseeing the set-up for the group, the words of the Zechariah Man began to echo in my mind once again.

I had not forgotten the word the Lord had imparted through that godly white-haired gentleman. In fact, Zechariah 4:6 had now become my personal scripture verse. But like many young preachers, I made the mistake of thinking I had fully learned this lesson the first time around. After all, I had received this word from an angel, hadn't I? (It is important when God speaks that we don't attach more honor to the messenger than we do the message. God does speak through angels, but He also spoke through a donkey.)

In order to help me begin to understand the importance of my relationship with Him, God was about to reemphasize the truth of Zechariah 4:6 one more time.

That winter evening, while I was watching the group prepare for their concert, Joel Chernoff, the lead singer of the group, came over to me and asked, "What are you so deep in thought about?"

When I told him about my previous encounter with the Zechariah Man, he began to smile with disbelief and interject funny remarks. I think he was trying to get me to loosen up a bit. He certainly knew that such experiences happened to people, but he just had trouble believing that it had happened to me. The more I tried to convince him, the more skeptical he became.

Finally, I said, "Joel, I'm serious. I was sitting here with my eyes shut and when I looked up, the man was standing right over there." I pointed to the left side of the sanctuary where, to my surprise, the Zechariah Man was standing once again!

I stammered, "Joel, that's him. That's the angel!" It was the same white-haired gentleman I had first encountered two years before. He looked exactly the same now as he had then.

The gentleman walked over and said, "Pastor, I was here two years ago and spoke a word to you. Do you remember what it was?"

I stood up straight and replied, "Yes, sir, it was Zechariah 4:6: 'Not by might, nor by power, but by My Spirit, says the Lord of hosts.'"

He looked deep into my eyes, as if he was looking into my heart and said, "Never forget this word!"

At that moment I began to cry. My heart was deeply pierced once more with the impact of those forceful words. You would think that one visit from God's special messenger would be enough, but God had sent His angel to me twice! This time, however, my heart was more fixed on the message rather than the messenger.

When the angel had finished, he turned to Joel and began to minister to him. Later, Joel came to me and said, "Craig, I'm sorry, I really had difficulty believing you, but after he was done talking with you, he spoke things to me only God could know." We were both trembling with amazement and awe.

What a way for the concert to begin! When the music started, the Zechariah Man was sitting in the same seat he had occupied two years earlier. This time I kept my eyes glued on him. The way he worshiped was such an inspiration to my heart—he seemed to literally glow with the presence of the Lord.

When the group paused halfway through the concert for the offering, I quickly glanced toward the platform and then back at the seat where the Zechariah Man had been sitting. As he had done at the concert two years before, the man had vanished from the premises! His mission had obviously been completed.

It was then that I knew the direction of my ministry was changing. In the days ahead, the Lord made it very clear to me that I was to start a new church and that the Zechariah Principle was to become the scriptural foundation upon which it was to be built.

Even to this day, I have never forgotten the message I received through that wonderful divine visitation: "Not by might, nor by power, but by My Spirit, says the Lord of Hosts." God went to great lengths to reveal that the spiritual provisions we all need to succeed in life will only come from Him. The work ethic I learned growing up, though valuable, could not even begin to compare with the work God desired to do in me, through me, and around me. Eventually I learned that this work must flow out of my relationship with the Father. I had now embarked on a journey to know Him in a way I had never done before.

Chapter Two

Searching for the Father

In the beginning, God created the heavens and the earth (Genesis 1:1).

There are essential truths regarding the Father that the Holy Spirit desires to reveal to each one of us. Let's go back to the beginning of Genesis: "In the beginning, God created the heavens and the earth" (Genesis 1:1).

"In the beginning, God!"—these four words say it all. Before the heavens were established, God was there. The Father was, is, and always will be. The world and everything in it has its beginning with the Father's actions. He is the Creator, Originator, and Founder, not only of this planet, but of all the other planets, stars, moons, solar systems, and galaxies, as well. All things found their beginnings through God the Father.

The verb *to father* is defined as, "To procreate offspring

as the male parent. To create, found, or originate. To attribute the paternity, creation, or origin of." The creation account, as it is recorded in Genesis 1 and 2, shows this definition in action, as we see the Father simply being Himself, the Creator. When God said in Genesis 1:26, "Let Us create man in Our image," He was establishing not only a biblical reference to the Holy Trinity, but also showing us the divine flow of authority under which the Godhead operates. In Genesis 1:2-3, we see this chain of command in operation:

> *The earth was without form and void; and darkness was on the face of the deep. And the Spirit of God was hovering over the face of the deep. Then God said, let there be light and there was light.*

The Holy Spirit was hovering (waiting) for the Word (Jesus) to be released by God (the Father). This is a perfect example of the unity of the Godhead. As creation is unfolding, we see the Word and the Spirit responding time and time again to the will of the Father. Notice I said *responding*, not reacting.

Action, Not Reaction

God never reacts, He only acts or responds. A reaction is usually a negative response to someone or something else that is seeking to take control. The American Heritage Dictionary defines "react" this way: "To act in opposition under the influence of a stimulus or prompting." Since the Father has all things under His control, how could anyone or anything have an influence over Him? At creation, when the Father acted, the rest of the Trinity responded.

God never wants us, as believers, to react to anything. We have been called to do what God does—to act or respond. That's why the fifth book of the New Testament is entitled, "The Book of Acts" and not "The Book of Reacts." At the gate called Beautiful, where the crippled man sat daily and begged for money, Peter and John didn't react to his disability, rather they responded to the man and his need. Peter looked him straight in the eyes and said, "I don't have any silver or gold, but I do have something to give you. In the Name of Jesus Christ of Nazareth, rise up and walk!"

Whenever we allow the Holy Spirit to take control over our lives, this enables the Father to act or respond through us as He did in the Genesis account of creation, and as He did through Peter and John. As we rise up in obedience to the Father's will for our lives, there is a release of glory that flows from His throne that will transform us and impact those around us.

I have always had a strong desire to please God so when the Lord directed me to start a new church in Lambertville, New Jersey (a small city of some 4000 people), our outreach and vision for growth slowly became all-consuming. We established a bus ministry to inner-city Trenton, and began to have special Sunday services geared toward reaching the needy. In addition, hundreds were fed Thanksgiving dinners and at Christmas, gifts were given to the needy.

We wrote and performed illustrated sermons and even held the area's largest Fourth-of-July spectacular, with music, skydivers, and a fireworks display. Although the motivation for each of these events and services was to reach people with the message of Jesus Christ, after each outreach I felt an aching emptiness deep within.

From my youth onward, as I mentioned earlier, I felt I never had the relationship with my earthly father that I desired. When Dad's walk with God suffered, so did the family. He was hardly ever at home, and when he was, his attentions were directed elsewhere.

Because of this, I would always strive for his approval. I felt if I were successful, then he would desire to spend time with me. I took his absence as personal rejection rather than seeing it as a man running from God. A father's approval is very important to his children and when this dimension is lacking, it creates an unsettledness in the heart of the child until this void is filled.

Without realizing it, I had allowed this same spirit of rejection to carry over into my ministry. I found myself striving for God's approval in the same way I had striven for my dad's approval. I did all I could to bring revival to our city. When my personal expectations for success were not met, I felt as if I had failed my heavenly Father. It seemed that I was always falling short of the mark, and deep within I felt I had not received God's complete approval.

A "Jesus Man"

I was raised in a conservative evangelical church home. At the age of 17 I was saved, and one month later I was baptized in the Holy Spirit, which was a bit irregular for a conservative evangelical. Even though over the years I had gained a tremendous sense of respect, appreciation, and love for the Spirit of God, I still considered myself to be a "Jesus man." When I prayed, it was to Jesus. When I worshiped, I worshiped Jesus. When I witnessed, I told others all about Jesus. I felt the sole purpose of the Holy Spirit was to promote Jesus and Jesus alone.

There were times when I remember hearing people praying to God the Father, and I would always think that they needed to become more intimate with Jesus, His Son. My view of God the Father seemed to be akin to the concept of an earthly father who retires and gives the family company over to his son. Even though I knew God the Father would always be there, I saw Him as a distant figurehead who was in the process of stepping down and handing the heavenly business over to His only Son, Jesus. I reasoned this way, *Why waste time praying to the Father when the new Owner is the one who can help you?* This is not meant to be disrespectful in any way; it simply illustrates that I had a limited view of the Godhead. My view of God had been greatly conditioned by my experiences with my earthly father just as my drive to succeed had been conditioned by his strong work ethic.

"Send Revival, Lord"

With this drive to succeed also came a deep desire to give God what I believed He wanted most—revival. However, none of the special events our church hosted had yet produced it. With this desire in mind, along with my wife and my two oldest daughters, I travelled to Florida in order to visit a particular church that had been experiencing a full-fledged revival for many months. I wanted to see and experience first-hand what everyone had been talking about concerning the move of God this church was experiencing.

We went directly to the church only to find a seemingly endless line of people who were awaiting entrance to the sanctuary. I had never seen Americans stand in a line like this before except, perhaps, for a rock concert or blockbuster movie. The amazing thing was that the long line had formed for a regular weekday evening service. The average church might have only one-tenth of their congregation at such a service, but at this church, thousands were waiting to enter!

Another surprising thing was that the attraction wasn't a

big-name celebrity or musical group. It was simply people who were hungry for more of God, and they had come to this place from all over the world to have that hunger filled. Like all the others, I was hungry to be filled as well, and excited to be in a place where God was obviously meeting so many needs.

As soon as I entered the sanctuary, God's presence was evident. There was an expectation in the hearts of the people that electrified the spiritual atmosphere. When the music began, it was as if a surge of energy had been released into the church, even though the songs weren't any different from what we sang at our home church. The sermon wasn't a grand demonstration of polished preaching either, it was just a simple message on repentance. But when the altar call was given, there was not enough room to accommodate the number of people who responded. Men and women, young and old, were weeping and repenting before the Lord. This church had what I wanted, and they had it without hype and hoopla. As I observed the impact of God's presence, the Holy Spirit reminded me again of Zechariah 4:6, "Not by might, nor by power, but by My Spirit, says the Lord of hosts."

If having big events headlined with big names and backed by big money were the secrets to building God's kingdom, then all of our cities and churches would have experienced a heaven-sent revival a long time ago. Even tragedy will not produce a long-term spiritual awakening. During times of war there were numerous "foxhole conversions." In the midst of the bullets and bombs, soldiers would cry out from their precarious positions, "Lord, if you deliver me from this, I will serve you forever." Unfortunately, once they arrive safely back home and resume their normal routines, most of them forget their battlefield prayer. Look at the tragedy of the New York Twin Towers terrorist attack on September 11. It produced more of a patriotic revival rather than a spiritual transformation. Surprisingly, statistics now show that church attendance one year after this terrible event is less than it was prior to the attack.

However, when the Father builds the house, He also maintains and provides for it. Revival isn't about one or two particular churches having fantastic meetings; it's about people in every nation on the face of the earth coming into a close relationship with the Father who desires to pour out His Spirit on them. Man can't provide for something this big, only God can.

Revival isn't always what we expect. In fact, revival will destroy anything that is man-made. The Father is the Master Builder; He is the author and finisher of our faith. When we operate out of a close relationship with the Father, our labors are never in vain but will bear much fruit.

Modern-Day Example

The fruit of a godly father/son relationship can be seen, for example, in the relationship of Matthew Barnett to his father, Pastor Tommy Barnett. I remember when the vision for the Dream Center (Los Angeles International Church) was launched at Tommy's Pastor's School in 1994, when thousands of pastors in attendance responded with their support.

As Tommy continued to share his vision, churches, religious organizations, businesses, and individual supporters began to sow their finances and labors into the Dream Center. As the new church continued to gain momentum, the big question in everyone's heart was, "Who will pastor this church?"

Tommy made it very clear that God had shown him that he would finish his days at Phoenix First Assembly of God. In view of this, who could be trusted to carry out the vision he had received from God some 40 years before? (While visiting the United Nations in New York City as a young man, the Holy Spirit had birthed in his heart a church for all nations.) Now, by God's divine directive, the hour for this vision to be fulfilled had come.

The honorary board members of the Dream Center were chosen, including Willie George, Charles Neiman, Jack Wallace, E.V. Hill, Jack Hayford, and myself. Staff positions were being filled, with the Master's Commission assisting in evangelism and discipleship, but still no pastor had been chosen. Tommy needed someone who would respond to his vision for Los Angeles. At the time, Tommy did not know that the Holy Spirit had been dealing with his son Matthew's heart about the ministry in California. Matthew was only 19 years old, a young man by the world's standards, but the perfect choice by God's standard. The rest is history now.

A great work has been birthed in Los Angeles and it continues to grow. This was all because of a son's response to his father's heart for a hurting and dying people. Does this sound familiar? In the same way that Matthew went to Los Angeles to help fulfill the will of his earthly father, Jesus came to earth to fulfill the will of His heavenly Father.

We're no different than Matthew when it comes to the plans and purposes of God. He's our heavenly Father too! There is a destiny that has been prepared for us to fulfill. We may not have discovered our destiny yet, but it will happen if we seek the Father's will with all our hearts! The Father always honors obedience. God spoke through the prophet Samuel, "To obey is better than sacrifice." Obedience is the key that unlocks all doors. The door to our destiny will be unlocked when the key of obedience to the Father's will is inserted into the cylinder of our lives.

God would answer my prayer for revival, but little did I understand the difficult process that would be involved.

CHAPTER THREE

The Will of the Father

Father, if it is Your will, remove this cup away from Me; nevertheless, not My will, but Yours, be done (Luke 22:42).

Doing the Father's Will

Jesus understood the importance of doing the Father's will, even when He was about to go through the darkest hour of His life. For the first time ever, He would be separated from His heavenly Father. The anguish He had to walk through prior to His crucifixion must have seemed unbearable. On the night of Jesus' agony and betrayal, while He was praying in the Garden of Gethsemane, He cried out,

> *Father, if it is Your will, remove this cup away from Me; nevertheless, not My will, but Yours, be done"* (Luke 22:42).

This prayer illustrates the divine flow of authority displayed in Jesus' obedience. Once we understand God's position as Father, His purpose and ways become real to us. We find ourselves responding to Him and acting on His behalf in establishing His will on earth as it is in heaven. Jesus instructed His followers to pray,

> *Thy kingdom come, Thy will be done in earth as it is in heaven* (Matt. 6:10).

What is the will of the Father? What kingdom has He purposed to be on earth as it is in heaven? Everything the Father does has a purpose. Nothing is by chance because God always has a plan. Actually, He has only one plan because His ways always succeed. I have heard it said, "If plan A fails, God always has plan B." I don't believe this at all! If plan A does fail, it's because it was *our* plan, not God's.

Revelation 3:7-8 proclaims,

> *And to the angel of the church in Philadelphia write, These things says He who is holy, He who is true, He who has the key of David, He who opens and no one shuts, and shuts and no one opens. I know your works. See, I have set before you and open door, and no one can shut it.*

When God opens a door, no one can shut it, and if God closes a door, no one can open it. No matter how powerful we may be, no matter what resources we may have at our disposal, no matter how great is our sphere of influence, we can't speed up, slow down, or even stop the will of the Father.

When God shut the door of Noah's ark, it remained shut until He opened it. If we start trying to break a door down when God has closed it, we may find ourselves falling 20 stories into the swirling waters below!

Closed Doors Prepare the Way

A few years after we began the church in Lambertville, a married couple, who were among the greatest financial supporters of the ministry, had requested a special meeting with me. Three days prior to my meeting with this couple, the Holy Spirit came to me in a dream to prepare my heart for what I was about to experience. In this dream I was dressed in fine clothing and quality jewelry. Then, in an instant, I saw the jewelry disappear and my clothes turn to rags. While this transformation was taking place, I was instantly flooded with feelings of fear and panic. The anxiety so overwhelmed me that I was immediately awakened out of a sound sleep. I asked the Lord to show me what this meant. At that moment, I knew in my spirit that the upcoming meeting with our two supporters was not going to be a positive one. The Holy Spirit was preparing my heart to hear whatever they had to say.

For quite some time, this couple's financial support had played a major role in all of the evangelistic outreaches of our congregation. In fact, their tithes had accounted for 50 percent of the operating budget of the church. When they joined our fellowship, I was astounded by the amount of their giving and deeply grateful for their generosity. Lambertville Assembly had never experienced financial blessings at this level before. After watching this pattern of giving continue for several weeks, I thanked God that we were beginning to accrue a financial surplus, but with this excess also came many questions. Would this be the couple's regular contribution to the church or was this a series of special offerings? If the amount they were giving was their tithe, we wondered if we should invest the increase in interest-bearing accounts or if the Lord was saying it was time to use this increase in giving for building the church staff and ministries.

With these questions in view, I met with this husband and wife who assured me that they would continue to give the same amount each month. After much discussion, the leadership unanimously agreed to sow the increase back into the church by hiring some needed staff. It's amazing what money can buy. With a spirit of excellence, we went forward and began the building process of acquiring new leadership for the youth, children's, education, and evangelism departments. As a result, a top-notch children's program was up and running, a youth ministry was set in place, a Bible institute was established, an active evangelism outreach ministered weekly to our community and the surrounding communities, a bus program was begun, missions giving was increased, and special evangelistic mission trips were planned. We even had to hire a bookkeeper because so much revenue was flowing through the church.

During this exciting time we were able to pay a second mortgage of nearly $700,000 in full. I always thought if I had the necessary finances, then the right people could be hired, the right ministries could be put in place, and then God would fill our church with people. This was only partially true. All of the above had taken place except the last expectation—our church was not yet full.

Yes, there was growth, and, yes, we were considered a large congregation, but it was not the kind of growth I had expected. On top of this, after three years of intense outreach, the church ministry had turned into a "money-eating machine." All of the ministry and money had failed to unlock heaven's gates over our city, and discouragement, discontent, and skepticism were settling into the hearts of the people. Unfortunately, the couple that had been such tremendous supporters of the church were now struggling with these same emotions.

Arriving at the appointed time for our meeting, the couple proceeded to share with me that the Lord had instructed them to leave our church. I asked them how they had arrived at such a decision. As they shared what they felt the Lord had placed on their hearts, it was obvious that they were certain they had heard from Him. I asked them when their departure would take place. After all, I had a large staff now, and these staff members would need time to find new jobs and relocate their families. The fact was that the loss of this couple's financial support would mean the loss of the additional pastoral and church staff positions we had added. There was no way the church could continue with the same obligations without the regular contributions this couple had been giving.

I hoped they would not leave for at least three months, or even after the first of the year. It was not to be, however. The couple said, "Pastor, we are leaving the church after this Sunday."

The finality of those words left me in a state of shock. I responded, "I have staff with families and this means that in three days they will no longer have a job or any source of income!"

The man answered, "I know, but this is what the Lord told us to do."

It was all extremely frustrating for me. The dream God had given me about the stripping of our financial support was unfolding before my eyes, and the future of my ministry in this church seemed to be coming to an end. But why did it have to end this way?

Well, it didn't. At first Satan tried to deceive me with his own interpretation of my prophetic dream. His interpretation was one filled with accusations and judgments, but after spending some time in prayer, I understood God was not punishing me. Instead, the Father had given me this dream in preparation for what was about to transpire. Looking back, I am also able to see how God was teaching me to focus on fulfilling His vision for my church and city, rather than instituting multiple programs in order to experience growth. I have found that it's one thing to draw a crowd and quite another to build a congregation.

As I entered this difficult time, the Holy Spirit often reminded me of the dream. Therefore, I took heart in the realization that if God cared enough to warn me about my future, He had already gone before me and prepared the way. I knew enough to understand that the key now was to keep praying and walking by faith and obedience along the path He had set before me.

We must trust the plan of the Father even when we don't understand it. He sees what we don't see, and He knows what we don't know. In Isaiah 55:8, God says,

> *For My thoughts are not your thoughts, nor are your ways My ways says the Lord.*

Yes, the Father has a plan and He has ordained that every blood-washed believer in Christ be a part of His magnificent purpose. It is important to understand the Father's position and purpose in our lives, or we will be distorted in our view of who He is and what motivates His heart. When we see the Father more clearly, our disappointments and problems become steps on the path toward a closer relationship with Him.

A Spiritual Purging Is Coming

Before the next great revival takes place, I believe we will experience a spiritual purging from church to church—a purging accompanied with a spirit of repentance. This purging won't be limited to one denomination. It will sweep through mainstream denominations, Pentecostal assemblies, independent churches, and conservative/fundamentalist fellowships alike—every church that desires to be used of the Lord. As recorded in Isaiah 6:5, people will cry out, "Woe is me, for I am undone! Because I am a man with unclean lips."

When God strips and cleanses us, we become more sensitive to His light. Imagine walking into a darkened room and sitting down. If you remain there long enough, your eyes will adjust to the darkness. But if someone comes along and turns on the light, it will hurt your eyes, and the brightness may actually cause you to cover your face. In such a situation your response to this will be either, "Turn that light off," or "Give me a moment so my eyes can adjust to the light."

Similarly, when God turns up the light of His glory, as He surely will, it will expose the areas of darkness within us. This experience will either cause us to run from His light back into the darkness or to embrace His light and remain in His presence, causing us to become more like Him. Such a spiritual stripping will unify us as God's people, an army with a single purpose and vision—His purpose and vision: "That the whole earth will be filled with the knowledge of the glory of the Lord" (Habakkuk 2:14).

During this time of purging, the church and I were going through much the same thing as Gideon did when God reduced the numbers of his army. God was reducing us by stripping our army financially and numerically, and it really hurt! Money was scarce, workers were scattering, and my vision was obscured. But through all of this, God was answering my heart's cry for revival. God was dimming my vision so I could embrace His.

In truth, I began to reevaluate everything I was doing, which is exactly what God wanted me to do. Even after releasing many workers from the church staff, our difficulties continued for more than a year. Day after day the changes in our church continued, and as all leaders know, people don't like change even when the result is good. Change is scary to many people because it directs them down an unfamiliar road and greatly disturbs their comfort zone. This is what happened in our church as well. Many people, including myself, felt quite insecure about what we were going through because we had never walked a road like this before.

The Way Out Is Through

During this time of tumultuous change, a large church in the Northeast contacted me about the possibility of becoming their next senior pastor. I was elated to know that this church was interested in me. I thought, *Finally, there's a way out of this mess!* (That's not an unusual first reaction when we are going through this process.)

Around this same time I even had people prophesy over me, "Change is coming and a door will open for you." Thank God, I had been taught biblical order with regard to such prophetic words. I knew that in the New Testament prophecy is never for direction, but only for confirmation. The prophetic word will confirm what the Holy Spirit has already personally revealed to us.

The devil, though, knew my flesh was looking for a way out of a difficult situation. It is during such times that we can be deceived into retreating from the process, rather than persevering through it. James writes,

> *If any of you lacks wisdom, let Him ask of God, who gives to all liberally and without reproach, and it will be given to him* (Jas. 1:5).

During this time, I earnestly sought God for wisdom, especially in the area of finances. He answered my prayer by showing me how to get the most for each ministry dollar. We examined every expense and cut all excesses.

Looking back on those challenging times, I realize that if I had accepted the job offer from the large church in the Northeast, I would have missed several key visitations from God that have proven to affect my life and ministry in so many crucial ways. Those circumstances would give me a new sense of direction that I firmly believe guides me now every day.

If we really want God to use us in a mighty way, we will have to endure the process of exchanging our name for His so that we can come into a close relationship with the Father. Paul declared how Jesus made Himself of no reputation. In other words, Jesus had no identity of His own. He didn't speak His own words, He spoke the words of the Father. He was so unified with the Father that He said, "He who has seen me, has seen the Father." Jesus lived to further the reputation of His heavenly Father.

Preachers often pray, "Lord, we want your glory," but there's a price to pay for that glory. Jesus was accused by religious leaders during His lifetime (as well as by modern-day critics) of being insane and demon-possessed, a crook, drunkard, womanizer, homosexual, false prophet, and even Satan, but He never let those accusations sidetrack Him but said,

*I have come down from heaven, not to do My own will,
but the will of Him who sent Me* (John 6:38).

During His trial and crucifixion, Jesus didn't speak a word in His own defense. Why? Because everything He did was done in order to fulfill the will of His Father.

Yes, there is a price to pay if we want to experience God's glory in our lives and ministries. Joseph walked through the fire with regard to what he faced as a result of the accusations Potiphar's wife had hurled at him, David walked through it with the house of Saul, and we walk through it today. God wants to bring us to the point where we lose all confidence in our good name. It is only then that we will begin to find confidence and protection in the Father's name and reputation. Once we reach this point, we are ready for the next level God has prepared for those who are willing to go the distance with Him.

All I went through, while definitely grievous at the time, was preparing me for a personal visitation with God the Father, and for that I shall be eternally grateful.

CHAPTER FOUR

The Father's Names

And God said to Moses, "I AM WHO I AM" And He said, "Thus you shall say to the children of Israel, 'I AM has sent me to you'" (Exodus 3:14).

A father who loves his children and seeks to be responsible is both a covering and a protection over them. Nothing describes this parental quality of God more fully than the Old Testament names of God. Each name declares a different aspect of His Fatherhood and vividly describes who He is. When you consider the role a father plays in the lives of his children, these Old Testament names will take on an even greater dimension. Through the various Hebrew names for God (listed below), we are able to gain dramatic glimpses into the nature and attributes of God as Father. This helps us to understand Him and to know His ways more fully.

✳ Once we understand who the Father is, our relationship with Him will deepen. During Jesus' earthly existence, He was still one with the Father. Look at what that oneness produced in His life and ministry. Jesus defied the laws of nature. He had authority over Satan and demons. Sickness and disease ran from His presence. People were restored to wholeness after spending time with Him. Sin's power was broken and removed from every person He forgave. The dead came back to life. The blind were made to see. Deaf ears were opened, and most importantly, people desired to have the same kind of relationship with God that Jesus had. That's the motivation behind every name we are looking at—that we might have the same relationship with the Father that Jesus has always had. ✳

✳ Every name declares what God the Father desires to become in our lives. Even though the Jews had no concept of God as their Father, every Hebrew name for God we are about to look at reveals an aspect of the Father's heart in caring for His children. ✳

ELOHIM: *God of greatness and glory. God, the Creator, the omnipotent and sovereign God; God, the governing power.*

Isn't this an apt description of a father? The name of Elohim attributes to God the ability to reproduce. We also see authority as part of its definition, which deals with the right to govern over others. This too describes the role of a father. In my own household I have four beautiful daughters. Each of them was given life and creation through the seed of my loins. As they mature, I serve as the governing power providing oversight, provision, and protection.

JEHOVAH/YAHWEH: *Eternal God of righteousness, holiness, and revelation, and the ever-loving One.*

This name also describes the role of a father. First, a father should seek to live an exemplified life before his children. This would encompass righteousness and holiness. A father is also a revealer of truth to his children. And the love of a father is unconditional. He loves even when it's hard to do so.

I didn't fully understand this principle until I became a father. It's amazing how a child can rebel against their parents' authority and yet the parents' ability to love them goes unhindered. Our children can break our hearts, but they cannot break our love.

EL: *The strong One, the God of strength, or the mighty God.*

In the home, the father's strength imparts a sense of security to his child/children, causing them to know they are safe. As an earthly father provides safety and protection for his children, God, our heavenly Father, guards and protects us, giving us a wonderful sense of safety and security at all times.

My youngest daughter illustrates this example well. We were on vacation one summer when she was only seven or eight years old. Wherever I went, she followed so that I began to call her "Shadow." As time progressed, this behavior intensified until it became excessive. Finally I asked her why she would never leave my side. Her response was, "Daddy, you're big and strong and I know you will never allow anything bad to happen to me." In other words, she felt safe and protected by her father. These positive feelings caused her to desire to abide in my presence continually. This is how God's presence should affect us as His children.

JEHOVAH SHALOM: *The Lord, our peace, wel-*

fare, good health, prosperity, favor, rest, restitution and whole-ness.

The heart of God the Father is filled with peace. He wants peace for His children and peace on earth. Jesus came to do the Father's will, and He is called the "Prince of Peace." He also went about healing every manner of sickness and disease. Again, Jesus was fulfilling the Father's will. A father is concerned that his children be well-rounded or whole. Isn't it amazing how this name for God is reflected in the role of an earthly father? God has always desired to be a Father to His people. Maybe you haven't experienced this kind of relationship with Him yet, but if you draw near to Him, you will. He loves you!

EL SHADDAI: *The almighty, all-sufficient God. The God who satisfies. The God who is more than enough.*

Another responsibility of a father is to satisfy the needs and wants of his children. There is nothing that pleases a father more than when he knows he has sufficiently provided even beyond what his child expected. Philippians 4:19 says, "And my God [Father] shall supply all your need according to His riches in glory by Christ Jesus."

JEHOVAH ROHI: *The Lord, our Shepherd, feeder, keeper, companion, friend, pastor, and herdsman.*

As a shepherd, pastor, or herdsmen leads his flock, a father leads his family through life. A father is a provider and protector over his family and belongings. Looking back at Israel in the wilderness after their exodus from Egypt, we see God fulfilling this role throughout their 40 year pilgrimage. And when it comes to companionship, there is nothing more fulfilling than when a father and child spend time together. This is the kind of relationship God the Father, desires to have with mankind.

JEHOVAH ROPHI: *The Lord, our Healer; the Lord, our Physician; the One who mends, repairs, and restores.*

A father desires to make things better. When things are broken, children bring them to their father in order to have him mend, repair, or restore them.

I remember one situation when my children were younger, and one of my daughters was not feeling well. After giving her something to settle her stomach, she looked at me and said, "Thank you, Doctor Daddy."

Being "doctor daddy" was God's ministry to Old Testament Israel on several different occasions, and yet the Hebrew people never really entered into relationship with Him in this way. Therefore they struggled time and time again when faced with challenging situations.

We need to come to the place in our spiritual walk where we see God as being bigger than any situation we may face. David had this mindset when he faced Goliath. Caleb manifested this kind of spiritual vision and took possession of his mountain. Romans 4:17 states, "And (faith) calls those things which do not exist as though they did." God is a faith God. Each of His names reflects the many different ways His faith takes action.

When we fill our hearts and minds with the reality of His names, we begin talking and acting like the Father does. A renewing process takes place so that we view things the way He views them. Revelations about God's nature builds a strong foundation of faith that will position us strategically for the end time revival that is about to sweep through every nation of the earth.

Take a brief moment to skim through the following Old Testament names of God. It's not my intent to bore you with them, but rather to reveal to you the first person of the

Trinity in a way you've never known before and spark within you a desire to become more familiar with Him as a loving heavenly Father who cares for you. When we consistently fill our hearts and minds with the knowledge of who the Father is, we will become more like Him in our ministry, mindset, and mission.

ELOAH OR ELAH: The adorable or everlasting One. The God who is worthy of worship.

EL-ELYON: God most high. God, the high and lofty One.

EL ROI: The Lord who lives and sees.

ELOLAM: The God of eternity. The God who was, who is, and who will always be.

ADONAI: Jehovah, our Ruler; God, our Master.

JAH: The independent One, our Immovable and ever lasting refuge and defense.

JEHOVAH HOSEENU: The Lord, our Maker.

JEHOVAH NISSI: The Lord, our banner or standard.

JEHOVAH M'KADDESH: The Lord, our Sanctifier.

JEHOVAH TSEBAOTH: The Lord of the hosts of Jehovah.
JEHOVAH TSIDKENU: The Lord, our righteousness.

JEHOVAH SHAMMAI: The Lord is with me.

Are you beginning to experience the revelation of who the Father is? All of the Old Testament names of God help to describe Him to us. Jesus stated that He didn't come to perform His own works, but the works of the One who sent

Him. Everything Jesus did, including His miracles, wisdom, teaching, forgiveness of sins and unconditional love, were a direct representation of His heavenly Father.

✳ When Jesus responded to Phillip, "He who has seen Me has seen the Father," it wasn't the color of His skin, the length of His hair, or the style of His clothing that reflected the Father. Jesus was referring to the character, purpose, motivation, purity, power, and authority He displayed in His day-to-day life. ✳

The God of Restoration

I believe the world is about to experience the greatest move of God ever to sweep the face of the earth. God the Father is a God of restoration. The Scriptures reveal this to us. Look at Genesis 1:1-3,

> *In the beginning God created the heavens and the earth. The earth was without form and void; darkness was on the face of the deep. And the Spirit of God was hovering over the face of the waters. Then God said, let there be light and there was light* (NKJV).

Here we see God creating the heavens and the earth. (See Genesis 1:1.) Because God is perfect, whatever He creates is always created perfectly in its original state. That means the heavens and the earth had no imperfections, flaws, or abnormalities. Then, in verse two, we see the earth described as being formless, void, and covered with darkness. What happened between verse one and verse two? The first three words of verse two reads, "The earth was." The Hebrew word for "was" used here can also be translated as "became."

Now let's reread the verse with this definition in mind.

"The earth became without form and void; darkness was on the face of the deep." The word "became" shows transition or transformation, going from one condition to another. Theologians teach that after the creation of the heavens and earth in verse one, Lucifer, along with one-third of the angels, launched their attack against God in heaven as recorded in Isaiah 14. It was this revolt that caused the fall of Lucifer (Satan) and one-third of the angelic host (demons) from heaven down to the earth.

The moment their presence was manifested on the earth, it took on their fallen condition. The earth was now covered with darkness because the Prince of Darkness lived on it. In verse three, we see how God begins to deal with the earth's fallen condition "Let there be light, and there was light." By the simple release of His Word, the earth was restored from a place of darkness to light, from emptiness to fullness, and from death to life.

This is a very important principle to understand. God always finishes the way He starts, in perfection and strength. For example, through the plan of redemption He provided a way of restoration for man, and He will do it again by restoring His church to strength, unity, and power. The Father never ends anything on a negative note. and so a great revival will come. It would be out of character for the Father to end church history in any other way.

A Revival Is Coming!

There is a revival coming! The Father is about to restore His people, and then, at the right time, He will restore His creation. He will take us from darkness to light, emptiness to filling, and death to life. The purpose of this restoration is for the fulfillment of His plan.

He has assured us that the whole earth shall be filled

with the knowledge of His glory. Every knee will bow and every tongue will confess that Jesus Christ is Lord, to the glory of the Father. His will shall be done in earth as it is in heaven. We have been predestined as a people to rule as kings and priests with Jesus in the ages to come. Jesus is following the orders He has been given from His authority, the Father.

Therefore, if we are going to see this revival and experience this restoration, then an intimate revelation of God the Father has to enlighten us both individually and corporately. This revelation will take us into the Holy of Holies, where the manifest presence of God the Father abides. Our entire being will be saturated with an aroma from His manifest presence and this spiritual fragrance will totally transform our lives and enable us to carry His grace, mercy, and love to the needy.

If you want to understand the Father, His essence is summed up in 1 John 4:8, "God is love" (NKJV). The Father is love in its purest and most potent form. Therefore, understanding the Father means experiencing the fullness of His dynamic love.

CHAPTER FIVE

Fathers Under Fire

For we do not wrestle against flesh and blood, but against principalities, against powers, against the rulers of the darkness of this age, against spiritual hosts of wickedness in the heavenly places (Ephesians 6:12).

God's Master Plan

There is an unprecedented attack against fathers taking place all over the world. This assault is not new, but has been going on since the beginning of time. Many of us have been victimized by this attack, because Satan's battle plan utilizes various avenues of assault. For some it's a father's marital infidelity, eventually resulting in divorce, leaving a home wounded and broken as the innocent are left to pick up the pieces. Sexual child abuse is another attack that has marred countless sons and daughters, all because of a father's unholy cravings for sexual gratification. Physical abuse and abandonment have broken the hearts of children young and old, when a father who is to provide security and safety, winds up becoming the very one who threatens and violates this parental standard. Then there is the workaholic dad, who never has time for his family and the substance abusing father who emotionally never left adolescence and views life as one big party. I could go on and on. Fatherhood is under attack!

As the clock winds down on God's calendar for mankind, the onslaught will continue to increase because it is Satan's futile effort to try to stop God's master plan from being fulfilled. Scripture reveals that it has always been the Father's plan for man to experience with Him what Adam and Eve enjoyed before the Fall, and what Jesus experienced with Him before His incarnation, during His earthly walk, and now for eternity—oneness!

In John 10:30, Jesus said, "I and My Father are one." In John 17:11, Jesus also prayed,

Now I am no longer in the world, but these are in the world, and I come to you. Holy Father, keep through Your name those whom You have given Me, that they may be one as We are one.

There is a father-and-child relationship that God has ordained between Himself and mankind, and along with this desired relationship is an unquenchable yearning for fellowship that is motivated by the love He has for us. Through this divine relationship and fellowship, God the Father is able to reproduce supernatural offspring to carry out His eternal plan—a plan that will continue into the ages yet to come.

Although Satan cannot stop this plan from being fulfilled, he still tries. The current state of affairs in the modern-day home shows us the results of his evil handiwork. For example, the divorce rate for first-time marriages in the United States is 40 out of every 100 marriages, and the stats increase to 1.75 out of every two marriages for those who have been divorced and then remarry.

The outcome of this statistic is fatherless homes under the direction of single mothers. In *Fatherless New Jersey and Beyond* we read, "Over 19 million children in the United States live apart from their fathers. This represents 27 percent of all children." Research shows this produces a much higher incidence of crime, teen pregnancy, and child abuse.

In various regions of Asia there are fathers who are selling their children into slavery and prostitution for financial gain. For example, a father in Taiwan sold his 11-year-old daughter to a child pornography ring. The arrest of the buyers followed the confiscation of video footage showing this little sixth grade girl being brutally raped, and all because of the abandonment of her father in exchange for money.

Take a look at Australia as well. Historians have referred to this country as "The Fatherless Nation," a land that found its beginnings as a prison colony for England's undesirables, a place where the first free-born Australians didn't even know who their fathers were because of the prison sentence these men were mandated to fulfill. In many cases, the mothers of these children were estranged from their sons and daughters because they had embraced a lifestyle of prostitution in order to survive.

In the former Soviet Union, the abandonment of children by their fathers has become commonplace because of high unemployment and alcoholism. Other European countries have documented an increase of incest as well as violence in the home. In Kenya, Africa, 70% of the male population is under 21 years of age because of the devastating results of HIV and AIDS. What does this tell us? The devil is killing off the fathers of this nation through this insidious disease.

There is a spiritual war being waged against our fathers, but if we don't understand the strategy behind it, as Christians we will find ourselves overwhelmed and tempted to give up the fight.

A Distorted Perspective

Why is there such a concentrated effort to distort the world's perception of the father image? It's because our interaction and experiences with our earthly fathers will shape our concept of God as our heavenly Father. When this concept is distorted through abuse and rejection, man will refuse any kind of relationship and fellowship with God, especially one reflecting Him in a fatherly way.

It is for this reason that hatred and distrust towards God has filled the hearts of people worldwide. They blame Him for the atrocities taking place individually and corporately in our cities, they blame Him for the wars and famines plaguing third-world countries, and they blame Him for the awful diseases for which there are presently no cures. In a desperate search for answers, people look in every direction for relief, except toward God.

From the very beginning of time, Satan knew that God the Father had a desire for a family. Genesis 1:26-27 teaches that men and women were created in the image of the triune Godhead:

And God said, Let us make man in our image, after our likeness: and let them have dominion over the fish of the sea, and over the birds of the air, and over the cattle, over all the earth, and over every creeping thing that creeps upon the earth. So God created man in his own image; in the image of God He created him; male and female He created them.

Theologians agree that this is the first reference in the Scriptures to the Trinity. God the Father was speaking to God the Son and God the Holy Spirit.

Therefore, just as God is three and yet one, man was created as a spirit being, with the ability to communicate through a soul that lives in a human body. We reflect the godhead because we are three dimensions in one: spirit, soul, and body.

Look at 1 Thessalonians 5:23,

May the God of peace himself sanctify you completely; and may your whole spirit, soul and body be preserved blameless at the coming of our Lord Jesus Christ.

Paul describes the tripartite nature of man in this verse. In order for God's desire for a family to be fulfilled, mankind was given something no other part of creation possessed. Adam and Eve were given a human spirit. Animal and plant life, birds, fish and insects were all given their existence without that third dimension which only man possesses—the human spirit. This spiritual dimension opens the door for mankind to experience with God what no other part of creation will ever have—relationship and fellowship.

Intimacy With the Father

As I mentioned earlier, I have been blessed with four beautiful daughters. They are flesh of my flesh and bone of my bones. Nothing they do can ever cause them to cease from being my daughters. They could choose to hate me and disassociate with me, but they would still remain my offspring because we are related. My seed is within them. They belong to my family line. My relationship with my daughters is based on my biological role as their father. Whether or not they choose to be close to me is their decision, but it doesn't change the fact that I am their father.

Our salvation experience gives us a spiritual rebirth that enables us to experience a personal relationship with God the Father through the blood of His Son, Jesus Christ. His seed is then within us. We are His blood and belong to His family line. Whether or not we choose to be close to Him is our choice, but it doesn't change the fact that He has now become our heavenly Father. This is what it means to have a relationship with God. Once that relationship is established, fellowship can be enjoyed, and one of the ways this takes place is through worship.

Worshiping the Father

In the Greek, the word for worship is *proskuneo*. It is defined as, "To kiss. A uniting of two hearts." A kiss implies relationship and intimacy. Every evening my youngest daughter will smother me with kiss after kiss before she goes to bed. Her kisses are an expression of her love and relationship with me as her daddy. Because she chooses to spend time with me in such close fellowship, this act of intimacy can take place.

In the same way, man was created to have relationship and fellowship with God, our heavenly Father. The way we express this relationship is through fellowship expressed in acts of worship (spiritual kisses).

Genesis 3:8 records,

*And they heard the voice of the Lord God walking in
the garden in the cool of the day: And Adam and his
wife hid themselves from the presence of the Lord God
amongst the trees of the garden* (KJV).

Think about this for a moment. God came down and
walked with Adam and Eve in the cool of the day. Can you
imagine such an experience? There was such a oneness between God and man that they could literally take walks together. This is what the absence of sin produces.

In contrast, look at what was lost in fellowship with God
because of sin. In Exodus 33:18-20, we see Moses, a committed holy man of God, in the Tent of Meeting. A portion
of God's glory comes down, and it is during this time that
Moses makes a special request to God: And he said,

*"I beseech thee, show me thy glory." And he said, "I will
make all my goodness pass before thee, and I will pro-
claim the name of the LORD before thee; and will be
gracious to whom I will be gracious, and will show
mercy on whom I will show mercy." And he said, "Thou
canst not see my face: for there shall no man see me,
and live"* (KJV).

As faithful as Moses was, he could not experience, with
God, what Adam and Eve did in the Garden before the Fall.
Moses saw the back of God, but Adam and Eve saw His
face. Moses had a glimpse of God, but Adam and Eve could
look on Him continually. Life before the Fall is what God
always intended for mankind and Himself. Because of this
spirit-to-Spirit relationship, God experienced an intimacy
with man and man experienced an intimacy with God that
no other part of His creation had ever known—a face-to-
face relationship with Almighty God.

Spirit Speaks to Spirit

That's why Jesus told the woman at the well in John 4:24 that "God is a Spirit: and they that worship him must worship him in spirit and in truth" (KJV). In other words, Jesus was saying, "Spirit speaks to spirit." Without this dimension of the spirit, we could have no relationship with God or even worship Him. So Satan made it his business to attack the very first father, Adam. The purpose behind this attack was to break the relationship and fellowship that existed between God and man. The devil knew he couldn't remove the human spirit from man, so he decided to do the next best thing: kill it!

Because the devil knows God's Word, he knew if he could deceive man into disobeying God, then this would produce immediate spiritual death or death to the human spirit. The result of this spiritual death would be a breaking of relationship and fellowship between man and God.

The walks Adam and Eve once enjoyed in the Garden would be no more. The Father's glory they experienced face-to-face would be hidden from them, and man, who had once been the friend of God, would now become the enemy of God. The love and favor Adam and Eve enjoyed would be removed in an instant, and they would now be on the receiving end of God's wrath and judgment, rather than His grace and mercy.

The devil thought this would stop God's dream. There would be no spiritual reproduction from generation to generation. Sin would now be in the seed of the first father (Adam) and passed on to his children, his children's children, and so on. After the Fall, God spoke the following words to Adam, in Genesis 3:13:

And the LORD God said unto the woman, What is this that thou hast done? And the woman said, The serpent beguiled me, and I did eat (KJV).

God was not surprised by their disobedience. He has always known the beginning from the end. By asking this question, God the Father wanted Adam and Eve, and the generations yet to come, to know the severity of sin. He wanted mankind to hunger and thirst for this kind of relationship and fellowship again. He wanted us to know that no form of disobedience is worth losing relationship and fellowship over. He wanted to create in man an obedience that would never be shaken again.

An Act of Lavish Love

Because God is omnipotent (all-powerful), omnipresent (all-places), and omniscient (all-knowing), there was no need for Him to construct an alternate plan because of Adam and Eve's sin. He knew the Fall was inevitable.

Think about it for a moment. The first act of sin ever recorded in the Scriptures is found in Isaiah 14:12-21. Here we find a perfect creation (Lucifer), in a sinless environment (heaven), enjoying the fullness of God's glory in an atmosphere of continual worship. You couldn't have it any better, and yet in the midst of these perfect conditions, Lucifer chose to rebel against God.

Who tempted Lucifer? There wasn't any devil at this time, and yet this perfect creation, in a perfect environment, willingly chose to disobey God. It was not only Lucifer, but also the angelic hosts, which the Scripture states are without number. One third of the angels joined Lucifer's team in revolt against the Godhead.

Like Lucifer, these angels had been created without sin.

They lived in a sinless environment and they enjoyed the fullness of God's glory in an atmosphere of continual worship and yet they disobeyed God as well. What was their excuse? There is a pattern here in the decision-making process of creation.

It is a pattern we see again in Genesis 3, when Adam and Eve ate of the forbidden fruit. Like Lucifer, they had been created without sin. They lived in a sinless environment, and enjoyed the fullness of God's glory in ways no other part of creation had experienced, and yet they chose disobedience over obedience.

What was going on? Did God, the Creator, fail these three times? Of course not! God knew this pattern of disobedience would continue throughout all creation. Lucifer fell prey to it, one third of the angelic hosts were swept away by it, and Adam and Eve gave way to it.

Knowing this, God allowed the Fall to take place, so that at the right time, He could display the greatest act of fatherly love which would eternally impact the universe and creations yet to come.

The Missing Ingredient

This pattern continued to manifest itself in God's creation because there was one ingredient missing which would produce and manifest the necessary strength to resist disobedience. When God the Father sent His only Son to the world in the form of human flesh, within Jesus was the strength and power necessary to live in victory, free from all sin and disobedience. This strength and power was the residing presence of God the Holy Spirit.

Jesus was faithful to the end because He had something, or, I should say, Someone, that no other part of creation possessed—the residing presence of the Holy Spirit. You might be asking the questions, "Why didn't God place the Holy Spirit in Lucifer, the angels, and Adam and Eve right from the start? Wouldn't this have saved the world and God all of the heartache and sorrow of many centuries?" I had these same questions until God revealed to me how He (God), is bound by His own Word (law).

For You have magnified Your word above all Your name (Ps. 138:2).

I will hasten My word to perform it (Jer. 1:12 KJV).

Heaven and earth shall pass away, but My words shall not pass away (Matt. 24:35 KJV).

The word of the Lord endureth forever (1 Pet. 1:25 KJV).

Have you ever heard the statement, "My word is my bond"? This statement is emphatically true of Almighty God. The Scriptures teach that He is bound by His own Word. Hebrew 6:18 states it is impossible for God to lie. God also never changes His mind. He won't say one thing at one moment and something else under a different setting. People may be like this at times, but God is not like any man (see Numbers 23:19).

God's Word is His law, and so He (the Creator) could not place His Spirit within man (the creation) without the legal right to do so. When Lucifer fell, he fell by choice, not by deception. When one third of the angelic hosts fell, they fell by choice, not by deception. But when man fell, it came through a violation of God's law. Exodus 20:16 is God's command not to bear false witness or lie. When Satan came to Eve, he stole God's blessing from mankind through a lie. Look at what he told Eve in Genesis 3:4-5:

Then the serpent said to the woman, "you shall not surely die. For God knows that in the day you eat of it your eyes will be opened, and you will be like God, knowing good and evil."

This was a direct contradiction of what God had spoken to Adam and Eve. In order for Satan to have his way, he utilized deceptions and lies to cause man's fall. Man was deceived into disobedience, where as Satan and one third of the angelic hosts willingly chose disobedience. There wasn't any devil for Lucifer to blame his actions upon.

They chose sin, knowing the truth, but man chose sin, being blinded from the truth because of a lie. Satan had broken God's law, which means God then had the legal right to enforce the Law by taking whatever legal steps necessary in order to restore what had been stolen. Satan not only robbed man in the garden, but he also robbed God. Because of Adam and Eve's disobedience, they not only experienced separation from God, but God experienced separation from man as well. That's why when God put His plan of restoration into action, He made sure it was stamped with divine finality. Because our adversary was not a flesh-and-blood opponent, the only one who could break his power over creation was the Creator Himself and that's what He accomplished through the Cross.

The Cross is God's way of escape and restoration. When we feel trapped by our sins, there is a way of escape. If we feel our lives are beyond repair, God the Father is ready to do a mighty renovation. Sometimes negative thoughts of defeat and failure can have us believe we're finished, when, in reality, the only thing that's over is our failures. God's word to us is for new beginnings. We have the rest of our lives before us, we must place them in God's hands. Whether we're young, middle aged, or up in years, when we place our portions in the Father's hands, little becomes much. The loaves and the fishes of the young boy in scripture were multiplied once they touched the hands of Jesus. What began as a meal for a small group, turned into a feast for the multitudes. We need to place our failures in His hands. We must release our fears and doubts and believe the Word of the Lord for our future.

The reality of these truths would become evident in the days ahead for our church. The next challenge our church came up against would test our ability to trust our heavenly Father as never before.

God's Prophetic Words Unfold

"LambertVision" was an annual event hosted by our church at the end of each summer. It was a four-day conference that featured Christian speakers, celebrities, high-profile athletes, and musicians from around the world. It was a gathering that attracted people from every denomination. It had become a financial boon for us even though it had initially been a monetary challenge. Now as we prepared for the fourth conference, there was an unusual stirring in my heart regarding the event.

One afternoon during an extended time of prayer, the Holy Spirit spoke the following words, "This will be your last LambertVision. I am about to change the direction of this church." My heart dropped when I heard these words. I thought God had already changed our direction. My mind began to race with questions while my emotions went on a roller-coaster ride.

What did this word from God really mean? Was my ministry at Lambertville over? Did God have a new church for me to pastor? All of the breaking and stripping from the past had become quite wearisome, and now I was ready for some good old-fashioned prosperity! There had been many tears shed along the way, so I reasoned it was now time for us to reap in joy. But in spite of all my protests, God had spoken.

At this point, I decided I needed to take time to be alone with Him. All the distractions in my life had to be removed so I could hear clearly from the Lord. One thing I have learned over the past 24 years of ministry is, "Don't interpret God's prophetic words, let them unfold." In many ways, I felt like Moses must have felt when he was called up to the mountaintop. I knew that there was something specific God desired to tell me. All of the difficulties of the past year had prepared my heart to hear whatever He was ready to communicate to me. My spiritual ears were wide open, and my heart was ready to receive.

Canceling all appointments, I locked myself in my study so I could seek God's face through prayer and fasting. I had nothing else in mind other than hearing God's voice. After I spent several days in His presence, God began to speak. His first instruction was to shut down all big events. He told me I was to dedicate the entire next church year to seeking His manifest presence through prayer and discipleship. Further, the Lord said, as we sought Him, He would unveil His strategy for my life and the life of this church. At this point I realized that God would have nothing further to say until I had faithfully carried out these instructions.

With all this in mind, I announced to the leadership that this would be our last LambertVision and explained to them what the Lord had instructed me to do. Every leader was in agreement with this word, and when we shared this directive with the congregation, they stood with us as well.

The people were tired. Sometimes it's easy to become so caught up in ministry that we forget the One for whom the ministry is dedicated. Such a situation then grows into a beast that devours everything in its path, including our time, our people, and our finances.

The Manifest Presence of God

What God was about to birth in my ministry and in our church is what He desires to do for all ministries. The end-time harvest the earth is about to experience will not be the result of big names, big events, big money, big people, or big sanctuaries. The earth is about to encounter what the presence of God the Father can and will do.

I had previously been dependent on names, money, and programs rather than God to grow our church. Now I realized that if God was going to use me in this last day's revival, then my dependence needed to be upon the Father.

This same principle applies to every believer. If you want God to use you in this final outpouring, the end-time harvest, the greatest revival the world has ever known, then you have to give up your dependence on names, money, and programs as well. I understand how the anointing can promote a name, and I understand that money is necessary in order to operate a ministry. Likewise, I believe God gives us programs that will reach our communities, cities, states, and nation for His glory. However, we must always remember that the name, money, or programs are not our source— God alone is our source! Hebrews 11:6 declares,

> *But without faith it is impossible to please Him, for he who comes to God must believe that He is.*

God wants us to know He is the power and authority

behind the name, He is the source behind the money, and He is the creativity behind the program. Names come and go, money is here today and gone tomorrow, and programs change from generation to generation, but God never changes. In fact, Hebrews 13:8 proclaims, "Jesus Christ is the same yesterday, today and forever."

This revelation brought great deliverance to me. My ministry would no longer be built around the resources I possessed, whether great or small. Revival isn't about what we have, it's about who God is! If the move of God comes from big events, big money, and big names, then what are the small churches to do? Heaven-sent revival is available for the little churches as well as the big ones. This *rhema* (revealed word from God) brought to me a deeper sense of security and a greater determination to obey every directive God had given and yet I knew there was so much more to come. This was only the beginning.

CHAPTER SIX

Restoring the Father's Image

So I will restore to you the years that the swarming locust has eaten (Joel 2:25).

Fallen Fathers Produce Fallen Fathers

As we have seen, since the time of Adam, Satan has made it his purpose to distort the father image in the hearts and minds of people around the world. Like a swarming locust, he has attacked the character and integrity of earthly fathers with selfishness, leaving countless children wounded and bitter, only to grow into the exact replica of betrayal and abandonment by which they were victimized.

Fallen fathers produce fallen fathers. As Liberty Savard brings out in her writings,

The unmet needs, unhealed hurts and unresolved issues we all experience early on, if left undealt with, will be passed on from generation to generation, and they will carry over into every area of our lives.

This is what Exodus 34:7b is speaking of when God proclaims:

Visiting the iniquity of the fathers upon the children and the children's children to the third and the fourth generation.

That's the reason, even to this day, there is so much conflict in the Middle East. It really isn't a religious war, it's a family feud that dates all the way back to Isaac and Ishmael. Abraham had two sons, but only one would receive his blessing. Isaac was God's anointed one, whereas Ishmael was a compulsive act of the flesh because of Sarah's impatience. Instead of asking God for wisdom, Abraham eventually expelled Ishmael from the camp, leaving him to fend for himself. Can you imagine what this young man had to deal with emotionally? Abraham took the short-term solution, but in the end, it wound up becoming a long-term problem. Through Abraham's rejection and abandonment of Ishmael, the Jews and the Arabs have been at odds for thousands of years.

A father's rejection is a very deep wound. If this wound goes untreated, these same children will grow into the next generation of fathers and then find themselves taking the frustration of their pain and suffering out on their own sons and daughters.

I wish the negative influence of these fallen fathers stopped at the front door of their homes, but it doesn't. These same men fulfill the role of political fathers, spiritual fathers, academic fathers, and occupational fathers, shaping the values and character of society's next generation of leaders.

Apart from a divine restoration of the father image, this same spiritual decay that began in the Garden of Eden will continue from generation to generation. The negative effects of this condition are evident in our modern-day family unit, political infrastructures, churches, educational institutions, and even our current work ethic. The motives they manifest reflect a mind-set of getting, rather than one of giving. This is the exact opposite of the Father's heart. God is a giver! Everything He does is for others, not for Himself. A true father will deny himself in order to provide for his children, and that's what God, the Father, did for all mankind.

Father God Is a Giver

John 3:16 says,

> *For God so loved the world that He gave His only begotten Son, that whoever believes in Him should not perish but have everlasting life.*

This motivation of love set the Father's plan for restoration in motion and caused him to anoint the prophet Joel to prophesy His promise to restore years of damage caused by Satan's attack (the swarming locusts).

As mentioned earlier, from Adam on, fathers have been under fire. This devilish attack has been relentless because man was created in the image of God. Humanity was given a dimension that no other part of creation possesses, and that dimension is the human spirit. Therefore, every time Satan and his demon legions look at man they see a likeness of "Someone" that no other part of creation reveals. In other words, Satan sees the image of God in every human being who walks the face of the earth. It doesn't matter whether a man or woman knows the Lord, he or she is still a spiritual replica of the living God.

The worst criminals who have given their lives over to crime by embracing evil even display the image of God. This image is not visible to the natural eye; it cannot be detected by the color of our hair, body weight, or even the natural abilities we possess. This image is a spiritual image, and is visible only in the realm of the spirit.

From the time of Adam forward, this image has been passed on from generation to generation and gives us dominion over animal life. It's the reason man possesses a garden instead of the garden possessing him. It's why "dog shows" are run and judged by men, rather than "man shows" run and judged by dogs. The movie, "Planet of the Apes" is Satan's fantasy of how he would have humanity view itself. The fact is, this kind of dominance by animals over human beings has never happened and it never will.

It's not the size and strength of creation that brings dominion. If this were the case, elephants and hippopotami would rule the world, and dinosaurs would have never become extinct. God gave this dominion and authority to man, not based on how big or powerful he is, but because of whom he was created to represent.

We are created in the image of God! That's why Satan will never truly embrace any human being as his friend. No matter how good or evil we choose to be, when Satan looks at man he will always see God and remember the war in heaven he lost. He remembers his fall to earth, the glory he once lived in and radiated, and his failure and soon-coming doom and destruction.

That's why the devil is obsessed with death. He wants to

remove that constant reminder of God from the face of the earth so he advocates war, murder, abortion, terrorism, and suicide in order to accomplish this end result. Satan hates man, but he has so twisted the truth that he has humanity thinking God hates man. Therefore the first step towards restoring the Father's image was for Him to send His Son, Jesus, the exact representation of the Father in character, motivation, and heart.

Look at what Jesus says in John 14:8-10:

> *Philip said to Him, "Show us the Father and it is suffi-cient for us." Jesus said to him, "Have I been with so long, and yet you have not known Me Philip? He who has seen Me has seen the Father; so how can you say show us the Father? Do you not believe that I am in the Father, and the Father in Me? The words that I speak to you I do not speak on My own authority; but the Father who dwells in Me does the work."*

Because the Holy Trinity is three and yet one, what is true of one part of the Godhead is true of each part. God the Father, God the Son, and God the Holy Spirit, always agree! I had a sincere sister in my church years ago who said to me, "Pastor, I had a supernatural experience and this is what I believe happened to me. I know this goes against Scripture, but the Holy Spirit bore witness to my spirit that it is true."

As convinced as this woman was, it didn't change the fact that she was embracing an interpretation of her experi-ence that could not be supported with the Word. I'm not saying she didn't have a supernatural encounter, but I do believe we need to weigh every experience we walk through against God's unchanging Word. Our experiences don't authenticate God's Word; God's Word authenticates our experiences.

1 John 4:1 states:

Dear friends, do not believe every spirit, but test the spirits to see whether they are from God, because many false prophets have gone out into the world (NIV).

The truth of the preceding verse shows us how Satan has been able to distort the world's view of God. Instead of judging God's character by His written Word, people often judge God by their personal experiences and disappointments.

People who try to rationalize their way through irrational circumstances will never come out with a proper concept of who God the Father is or what motivates His heart. Think about it for a moment. How could the *finite* mind of man ever understand and explain the *infinite* ways of Almighty God? Every attempt to do so would come from our personal perspective, which is crippled by a lack of understanding due to a limited view of the entire picture.

The Bridge of Restoration

Each one of us is vulnerable to deception and so God gave us His Word, and the Word (Jesus) was made flesh. The Word protects us from the lies of the devil. How else would we know the difference between truth and error unless there was a standard by which we can measure it? After the Fall, attention was taken away from God and focused on everything except Him. People continued to worship, but unfortunately for many, their worship centered on the creation rather than the Creator. That's why the Father sent His only Son. Jesus came at the appointed time to reveal the

Father once again to a lost and dying world. The cross became the bridge of restoration, taking man from death to life, darkness to light, sinfulness to righteousness, and bondage to freedom.

Through the cross, Jesus did not provide *a* way, but *the* way of restoration between God the Father, and man. The great revival that is about to come cannot and will not come apart from this restoration between God and man. Satan has established many strongholds in the hearts and minds of men, but through this revelation of the Father that Jesus is bringing, these strongholds will be torn down.

✴ The father of lies is about to be silenced by the unconditional love and truth of our heavenly Father. Fear, doubt, unbelief, and condemnation will be exposed and destroyed by the faith, confidence, belief, and mercy of our God. No sin will be beyond God's reach and deliverance in the minds of mankind, and no sickness will be too difficult for God's healing power.

It's Not About Men, It's About Him

After I announced God's new direction for our ministry to the congregation, a gentleman in the church approached me and asked if I would like to attend, at his expense, the next World Congress being held in Sao Paula, Brazil. Dr. David Yonggi Cho, Claudio Freidzon, and many others who had experienced God's manifest presence would be ministering to those attending this wonderful gathering.

I was both excited and humbled as I contemplated attending such a great event. Just the invitation alone filled my heart with gratitude to think that God had remembered me in this way. I happily accepted the man's kind offer, while sensing, at the same time, a part of my destiny was about to unfold. During my daily prayer time leading up to the trip, I began to experience an overwhelming sense of God's presence, which would leave me in a state of brokenness and tears. Day after day the same thing happened until the days turned into weeks.

One evening while in prayer, I asked the Lord why this weeping occurred each time I prayed about Brazil. God responded immediately by speaking the following words: "While you are in Brazil, I will place something in your hand, and what I place there you will carry to the nations. You will be a carrier."

When the Holy Spirit spoke those words, my heart broke in His presence. The tears I cried came from the depths of my spirit. I don't remember how long I lay there on the floor; I didn't want that moment to end. Actually, I believe if my spiritual eyes had been opened at that time, I would have seen angels ministering to me as they did to the Prophet Elijah. One thing was for certain—I knew I was being prepared for a divine encounter.

The World Congress in Brazil

Time passed quickly prior to my departure for the World Congress and soon I arrived in South America. It was so exciting to be there. Like many others, I had heard about the wonderful revival that was taking place in Argentina and Brazil, but now I would be able to experience it firsthand with my brothers and sisters.

The Holy Spirit kept recalling God's prophetic words spoken weeks earlier to me in prayer, "I will place something in your hand, and you will be a carrier." I wondered how this would happen and eagerly awaited what He was going to do. In what way was I to be a carrier, and to what nations? It was all so intriguing, but the harder I tried not to think about these things, the more my mind would race.

Therefore, I quietly prayed, "Holy Spirit, please help me steady my mind on other things" and was I amazed how God changed my train of thought so quickly!

As the week progressed, I was privileged to hear anointed speakers from around the world. It was as though I'd died and gone to heaven! I was awed to see so many Christians all in one place. The arena sat 15,000 people, and the stadium next door was set up to accommodate an additional 100,000.

Night after night both these facilities were filled, but the evening I remember most was when Claudio Freidzon was scheduled to speak. The bus from my hotel left an hour earlier than normal in order to beat the crowds, but the traffic was still unbearable. People and leaders from neighboring countries, as well as the citizens of Brazil, had come to hear this powerful man of God.

We disembarked from our bus several blocks away and walked the remaining distance to the arena. When we finally reached our destination, we were greeted by military police officers armed with machine guns, instructing us to leave. They kept shouting, "The crowds are too large, you must go home."

Where was I going to go? My bus was nowhere to be found and home for me was 5,000 miles away. I started to get angry. God had spoken to me prophetically that He was going to put something in my hand and that I would be a carrier. Here it was the end of the week, and nothing like that had happened yet. I was convinced that this was to be my night and that Claudio Freidzon was the man who would pray for me, but now it seemed that Satan had sent the Brazilian military to prevent me from receiving my blessing.

The moment we allow our emotions to take over, the

devil becomes larger than God to us. It was then I heard the Holy Spirit say, "Calm down, son, or you will miss what I am doing." I had temporarily forgotten that when God has ordained a visitation for us, nothing is going to keep Him or us from that divine appointment—not even the Brazilian military!

I prayed, "What do you have for me tonight, Lord?" When I turned around to consult with some of the pastors I was traveling with, one brother who had arranged for me to preach in a local assembly on Sunday morning, spoke up and said, "We will never get in this place. The church you'll be ministering in this Sunday is having a service tonight. Should we worship with them instead of attending here?"

My first reaction was a negative one because I thought my blessing was going to happen inside that arena, but God spoke to my heart and said, "It's not about men, it's about Me."

Without hesitation, I said, "Let's go!"

Forty-five minutes later we arrived at a small church in Sao Paulo. In Brazil, a small church is one with about 500 people, and that was the approximate size of this relatively new congregation. You could hear music coming from their building five blocks away! Even though I didn't understand Portuguese, I could sense their spirit.

The pastor was thrilled to see me, and the people greeted me as if I were a king. I soon discovered that Brazilian believers are very gracious people. It is obvious that an important part of their life is their service to others.

The pastor introduced all of us to his people and then continued the worship service. The music was wonderful. Percussion and brass instruments, along with guitars, keyboards, and drums filled the room with spiritual excitement while the people sang with all their might. Suddenly the disappointment I had felt over missing the Claudio Freidzon meeting disappeared. The Holy Spirit was obviously present in that small church, and little did I know what He was about to bring to me.

After the service, the pastor invited all of us upstairs for food and refreshments. We sat in his study while the ladies of the church set the table in preparation for a fantastic meal. During this waiting period, I noticed two women who were standing in the doorway and obviously trying to get my attention. I asked one of the Brazilian brothers with me what they were trying to communicate.

He responded, "They feel God has given them a word for you and are asking your permission to share it."

At this point the pastor rejoined us, so I turned and asked him, "Do you know these women?"

He replied, "Yes, indeed, these ladies oversee my inter-cessory prayer ministry and are two of the most powerful prayer warriors in my congregation."

At first glance, there was no inkling of the dynamic anointing within these two women. To the natural eye, they were extreme opposites. One was around six feet tall and the other barely pushing four feet.

Because the pastor had put his stamp of approval on them, I quickly forgot about the language barrier and waited for God to speak to me through them. With my hands lifted and heart wide open, I was ready to receive whatever God had in store. Humbly, the women came forward and placed their hands on me. The instant the little woman began to pray, a sensation like an electrical current started to surge through my body. Indeed, the Spirit of God hit me so hard that He almost knocked me out. I had never before experienced anything like it. The glory of God had entered that pastor's study and He had my undivided attention. Even though I didn't understand the language, I could sense when this precious intercessor moved from prayer to prophecy because the authority level in her voice rose to an even greater intensity. The anointing was so strong that I felt like my body was about to explode! To say I wept is an understatement. I was crying a river—a torrent of tears that seemed like it would not stop.

All I wanted to do was to repent in the presence of Almighty God because His holiness became so real to me. When the sister stopped prophesying, the taller woman took my hand in hers, opened up my fingers, placed something in my hand, closed my fingers again, and then patted my hand as if to say, "It's done!"

I thought she had probably placed a note there. When I gained my strength and composure, I opened up my hand to see what was there. When I did, I was amazed to see it was empty! At that moment the Spirit of God spoke to my spirit and said, "I told you I would place something in your hand and you would be a carrier; it's done!"

I had thought His blessing would be found in the arena with Claudio Freidzon, but God had arranged another visitation on the other side of town. Isn't that just like the Lord? He has His way of taking our eyes away from men and placing them on Him.

Later, when I received the translation of the prophecy that was spoken over me, I was astounded. It addressed in detail a legal issue I was facing and declared God's provision to meet that need. The prophetic word spoken through the little Brazilian lady also confirmed what the Holy Spirit had spoken regarding this visitation and my future ministry.

After arriving back in the United States, it was obvious to everyone that, like Moses, I had been to the mountaintop and met with the Father. I shared the entire experience with my congregation and they were thrilled. After recounting this experience, the big question many asked was, "Pastor, what do you think it was God placed in your hand?"

At that time, I honestly didn't know, but one thing was for sure, I had changed. It wasn't until two years later that God finally revealed what He had placed in my hand.

Jesus' Ministry to Mankind

The ministry of Jesus to mankind is that He is the way, the truth and the life (see John 14:6.), and to everyone who will say yes to His invitation, He will take them to meet the Father. Jesus was the exact representation of the Father in human form. That is why Jesus was given the title, "Christ." Christ is not the last name of Jesus, but rather it is the title declaring by what authority He was able to speak and do what He did. The word Christ, in the original Greek, is defined as, "The anointed one, anointer or anointing."

Paul said in Philippians 2:5, "Let this mind be in you which was in Christ Jesus." Jesus ministered with the mind of Christ, or the mind of the Anointing. When we enter into this same mind-set, the Anointing will then serve us as it served Jesus. The Anointing acted as the doorway of access to the Father where the glory abides.

Every time Jesus healed the sick, the glory of the Father was released. When the demon-possessed were delivered, the glory of the Father was revealed. When Lazarus was raised from the dead, the Father's glory was manifest. The Anointing is the key that unlocks the door to the Father; and where the Father abides, the glory abides as well.

When the Father's glory is released, it corrects the distorted mind-sets people have about Him. I believe the greatest injustice God has experienced is the intellectual stripping away of His love. First John 4:8 states, "God is love."

Truly, the Father has gotten "a bum rap." He didn't come with a whip, but with healing in His hands. God the Father is not responsible for all of the abuse earthly fathers may have inflicted upon their children. The truth is, He wants to bring healing and restoration to these same hurting people and the way we can receive it is by seeking and remaining in His presence. When this happens, the benefits of God will take control of our lives.

I remember one particular Thursday evening service at our church. During the praise and worship, an elderly woman suddenly lost consciousness. After attempting to check her vital signs, her son abruptly yelled out, "Call 9-1-1, my mother just died!" This quickly became no ordinary service. There was a spirit of expectancy flowing within the hearts of the people, and now everyone was waiting to see what God would do next. Before we could even pray, the woman sat back up and regained total consciousness. God's glory was so strong in our sanctuary that death had lost its ability to produce its final verdict. How powerful are the blessings of the Father!

The Father's Blessing

My wife and I have four daughters—Kelley, Heather, Heidi, and Laura. As an earthly father, it is my desire for all of them to experience my blessing. Keeping this in mind, every Saturday in the Lauterbach house is set aside as "Project Day." With each new project also comes a list of supplies I will need to pick up at the local home improvement center.

As I am preparing to leave the house to purchase the supplies I'll need, Laura, my youngest daughter, predictably comes running out and shouting, "I'll go with you, Dad!"

I thank God that I have a good relationship with all my

children, but what healthy, warm-blooded, fun-loving American girl wants to go to a home improvement center filled with tools, machinery, hardware, and construction equipment, especially on a Saturday morning when she could still be sleeping?

The answer is simple. Laura knows there is more to the Saturday morning outing than just the home improvement center. Experience has taught her that if I stop at the local restaurant for breakfast, she gets breakfast too. If I stop off to shop at a sporting goods store, she will leave with an item as well. There are many unexpected blessings involved when she chooses to have fellowship with Dad, and the same principle applies when we choose to have fellowship with our heavenly Father. Psalm 103:2 says, "Bless the Lord, O my soul, and forget not all His benefits." There are benefits for those who learn to abide in the Father's presence.

Earlier I listed and defined several of the Hebrew names for God. Each one describes a different aspect of God's character. The more time we spend with God the Father, the more like Him we will become and the more we will experience the attributes of His personhood first-hand. It has often been said that we begin to take on the attributes of the people that we spend the most time with. If we abide in God's manifest presence long enough, we will become like Him. In fact, His very aroma will surround us.

One brother in the Lord whom I knew years ago loved a certain popular men's cologne. The only problem was that he didn't just spray it on; it seemed as if he literally bathed in it. If you walked into a room he was in, you'd walk out smelling just like him. Wherever he went, you knew he had been there because you could smell his presence.

In a similar way, when we have been in a room that is saturated with the glory of the Father, we will walk out smelling just like Him. The longer we stay there, the longer the glory will remain on us. Remember, His glory is who He is and His names are descriptive of His glory. This means that the longer we abide in His glory, the more glory we will benefit from in our spiritual walk, ministries, relationships, and personal provisions.

Laura understood this truth from a natural perspective, and in this same way, God is challenging us as believers to understand it from a spiritual perspective. When we are saturated with the glory of the Father, His glory will bring transformation and restoration into every aspect of our lives, both public and private. Just as the Father's glory restores us, we, in turn, will become vessels of restoration in the lives of others. Then together we will march into the enemy's camp to take back what rightfully belongs to God. What a glorious day that will be!

CHAPTER SEVEN

The Apostolic Renewal

*Behold, I will send you Elijah the prophet, before the
coming of the great and dreadful day of the Lord. And
He will turn the hearts of fathers to their children, and
the hearts of the children to their fathers* (Malachi 4:5-6).

A Quest to Find Father

Several years ago, I became acquainted with a couple
who had four children. The eldest child was from the
wife's previous marriage and the three younger ones
were their own. From the beginning of their courtship, the
husband fully accepted the child from the wife's first marriage. After their wedding, he even adopted the child so they
would all have the same name. He loved this child as his
own and was always willing to go the extra mile, but in spite
of all the support, love, and quality time they spent together, there was a deep void in the heart of this child and

an insatiable longing to come to know their biological father. This desire was so overwhelming that it eventually led the child to embark on a quest to locate and meet the unknown dad.

What does this tell us? Even when we have the ability to provide the very best life has to offer, even when the proper time is spent together building a relationship, even when everything we know to do has been done, there is still a need within the heart of man to experience a unique father-child relationship. This principle is true, not only from a natural standpoint, but from a spiritual one as well. People deeply desire to have a relationship and fellowship with Father God. Just as we see this growing trend of adoptive children taking steps to meet their biological fathers, there is a spiritual hunger growing in the hearts of men and women worldwide to meet their heavenly Father and come to know Him better.

People no longer want to leave God out; they're opening their hearts and seeking Him. Pascal stated it correctly when he said, "There is within the heart of every man a God-shaped vacuum that only God Himself can fill." The stage is being set for a revival that will center around a revelation of God the Father. But before this happens, there will be an outpouring from heaven that will awaken spiritual fathers all across the earth.

A Full Fist

God is going to restore the position and ministry of spiritual fathers in church government with an apostolic renewal. In Ephesians 4:11, Paul mentions five different positions of ministry, which many have referred to as the Pulpit Offices: "And He Himself gave some to be apostles, some prophets, some evangelists, and some pastors and teachers." For years, three out of the five offices (teacher, pastor, and evangelist) have been the focus of the Church. People had no problem referring to someone as a teacher, pastor, or evangelist, but the moment an individual was given the title of prophet or apostle, the walls of resistance would go up.

I have heard the five-fold ministry referred to as a fist. What is the purpose of a fist? Normally a fist is used as an offensive weapon to strike with. The tighter you close the fingers, the greater impact you will have on what is being struck. Try making a tight fist while leaving the thumb and index finger out. Instead of a fist, it looks more like a gun. Next, try making a fist leaving only the thumb out. This is a little better, but still it's not complete. It's not until every finger is pulled together firmly that the fist can have the full impact it was intended to have.

This same concept is true of the five-fold ministry. The Body of Christ will never have the full impact the Father intended it to have until its spiritual fist is complete. Before the end-time harvest sweeps across the face of the earth, the ministry of the teacher, pastor, evangelist, prophet, and apostle will be fully restored and functioning. Each of these offices serves a different purpose in equipping the saints to do the work of the ministry.

Apostles—Fathers of the Church

What is an apostle? The Greek word for apostle is *apostolos*. This biblical word is defined as, "Apostle, messenger, delegate, or one sent forth. The one sent was given full power of attorney to act on behalf of the authority they were representing." This term originated with the Roman Empire, and it was used to classify the specific duties of a Roman Navy Admiral. When Rome would conquer a new territory, they would follow their victory by sending a fleet of ships carrying a colony of Roman citizens to inhabit the new land. With these people, the navy admiral/apostle would establish Roman governmental rule in the new land by appointing and training leaders. Once the new government had proven itself by manifesting the appropriate stability, the navy admiral/apostle, as the founding father of that city, would then turn complete rule over to the local magistrates and depart for Rome where his next assignment would be awaiting him. In the same way that an admiral/apostle was the founding father of a city within the Roman Empire, a New Testament apostle is a founding father of a Christian church.

In the Scriptures we see two different classes of apostles mentioned. Look at Revelation 21:14,

Now the wall of the City had twelve foundations, and on them were the names of the twelve apostles of the Lamb.

This verse describes the wall around the Kingdom of heaven. On the base of each foundation a name is inscribed. The names we find here are the names of the twelve founding apostles (or fathers) of the New Testament Church: "The Apostles of the Lamb." These apostles were an elite group of men who physically witnessed Jesus' water baptism, His resurrection from the dead, and His bodily ascension into heaven. See Acts 1:21-22,

Therefore, of these men who have accompanied us all the time that the Lord Jesus went in and out among us, beginning from the baptism of John to that day when He was taken up from us, one of these must become a witness with His resurrection.

This is the one thing that set the "Apostles of the Lamb" apart from and above the "New Testament apostles." The Bible mentions many apostles, such as Paul, Andronicus, Junia, Apollos, James, Silas, Timothy, Titus, and Epaphroditus. These men were powerful in word and deed, but because they did not personally meet the criteria of an apostle set forth in Acts 1:21-22, they could not be given the title "Apostles of the Lamb."

New Testament apostles were part of the early church, and they are still necessary in the present age of ministry and hold the highest office of ministry in the church. "And God has appointed these in the church: first apostles..." (1 Corinthians 12:28). A genuine apostle should manifest signs, wonders, and mighty deeds in his ministry. Paul wrote,

> *Truly the signs of an apostle were accomplished among you with all perseverance, signs, wonders, and mighty deeds* (2 Corinthians 12:12).

Apostles are church planters with good organizational skills for establishing local church government, and they know what it means to suffer persecution:

> *For I think that God has displayed us, the apostles, last, as men condemned to death; for we have been made a spectacle to the world, both to angels and to men* (1 Corinthians 4:9).

One other important truth to keep in mind is that apostles are never self-appointed. Those in positions of spiritual authority always commission apostles. We had a vivid example of the need for commissioning with an individual who briefly attended our church and prophesied the same message week after week. It was similar to the instance when the Apostle Paul had a damsel following him from place to place, exhorting people to listen to the words he spoke. It wasn't until the gift of discerning of spirits functioned in him that Paul was able to distinguish a bad spirit and take authority over the situation. It was the same with me as I sought God's will concerning this man and his prophecies.

One Sunday this man came in at the same time he always did, walked down the same aisle, sat in the same seat, and began to weep in the same fashion he had done for the past several weeks, and then he started to prophesy. The instant he opened his mouth, my spirit was grieved. It was at that moment the Spirit rose up within me and the following words came out of my mouth: "In Jesus' name, I forbid you to speak!"

This man couldn't believe his ears. He became flustered as my leaders ran to the front of the sanctuary and surrounded him. Before long, they proceeded to usher him out of the church. The song service resumed and I went to the lobby to see this man, along with my leaders. He was completely outraged! There was absolutely no reasoning with him.

I said, "If you will not come under my authority, I will be forced to place you under another authority."

His response to me was, "I'm an apostle! I answer to no one except God."

I countered, "Scripture teaches that even an apostle must come under the authority of the pastor in the local church."

The man still refused to cooperate, so the police were contacted and they escorted him from the premises. There is no such thing as a self-proclaimed apostle. In fact, I have found that when an individual has a genuine apostolic anointing on his life, people will recognize that calling and refer to that leader as an apostle without having to be told to do so. Many times, spiritually perceptive people will discern a person's calling even before the person with the calling does. Why is this the case? Proverbs 18:16 states, "A man's gift makes room for him, and brings him before great men". When God has elevated someone to the office of an apostle, those around the apostle will recognize the authority that goes with that office.

For example, Samuel recognized David's calling before David himself did. The same was true with Barnabas and Saul (who later became the Apostle Paul). Even when Jesus called the disciples, He believed in them before they believed in themselves. During the three years Jesus spent mentoring them, He focused on helping them grow into the spiritual fathers or apostles He had predestined them to be.

From the very inception of the Church, there were apostles (spiritual fathers). When the apostolic office is in place, God can establish and maintain His order because an apostle has been broken, shaped, and forged in order to both receive and give the very heart of the Father to others. True apostles are not interested in promoting themselves; they, like Jesus, have only one heartbeat—to do the will of their loving heavenly Father.

Spiritual Sibling Rivalry

The absence of an apostle's heart brings a spirit of competition into the church. We could call this "spiritual sibling rivalry." There is nothing that disturbs the heart of a father more than when his children fight with each other. Tempers flare, words fly, and fists swing as siblings compete. There always has to be a winner in such a conflict and even after one wins, the other devises how to get even.

Does this sound familiar? As I was growing up, my middle brother and I were always in competition and strife with each other. It didn't matter what it was—sports, music, or even practical jokes—sooner or later we would wind up in a fight. My mother would yell at us and try to spank us, but that didn't work. She cried tears of frustration, but that didn't work either. However, when she would say, "When your father gets home, he is going to skin you alive," we would stop in our tracks. Holy fear overcame us because we knew our father would bring order to the situation.

Because there has been an absence of apostolic or fatherly rule in the Church, the children of God have been in competition and strife with one another. They can't seem to tolerate one another's faults and weaknesses and don't have the patience to work with each other in church ministry. Just like our biological children, these spiritual children argue, backbite, and compete with each other. They want to be the pastor's favorite, or have the most effective ministry in the church. If anyone threatens such a person's place in the local body, the one who does so becomes the next target of their defensiveness and insecurity. This is what I mean by "spiritual sibling rivalry."

Do you know why this is happening in the church? It's because spiritual fathers produce spiritual fathers, but when there are no spiritual fathers in the church to bring order and to mentor the spiritual children, there will always be a divided church.

From Manhood to Fatherhood

As I mentioned earlier, my middle brother and I constantly fought with each other. Thank God, that's not true any longer. Someone might explain the difference this way, "It's because Jesus came and broke that demonic stronghold in your lives." Well, that's not the case. The simple fact is, we grew up! After my brother and his wife had their first child, there was a change in my brother. He wasn't the same person any more; he seemed more settled. His tolerance level had also grown so that he wasn't interested in competing with me any longer. He had made the transition from manhood into fatherhood.

A few years later, after my wife, Cindy, and I had our first child, I went through the same metamorphosis and made the same transition of crossing over from manhood into fatherhood. Because of this experience, the relationship between my brother and me also went through a transformation. As brothers, we had fought, but now as fathers, we stood together.

In the same way, it's time for the Church to grow up! The competition needs to stop. It's time for all of us to make that spiritual transition. It's time for the leaders to cross over from manhood to fatherhood in the Spirit. The Church is crying out for spiritual fathers (apostles). Fathers produce fathers. When the apostle's ministry is working, the Church will give birth to an apostolic people and an apostolic ministry.

It's this kind of Father's heart that will open the doors for revival. God's heart will change the hardest of hearts because He has not written off any sinner, including sinning saints! I believe when this end-time revival occurs, we are going to see the repentance of some people whom we thought would never repent.

The truth is that God is going to knock down every barrier that stands in the way of spiritual restoration. The overriding theme behind this outpouring will be the Father's love. If my children make a mistake, it breaks their heart at times to think they let their daddy down. Why is it, then, that they come and confess their failure to the one they feel they've disappointed? It's because, beyond their mistake, they see a heart of love in me that is willing to forgive them and to help them unconditionally.

Apostles or spiritual fathers will manifest this same unconditional love that will, in turn, produce what God the Father desires—unity! When the office of apostle is established and functioning as God has always intended it to do, a spiritual replication of this apostolic mantle will begin to fall and spread throughout the Body of Christ. Spiritual parents will begin to rise up and fulfill their purpose. The process of spiritual maturity will be set in motion. Newborn babes will mature into children, and children will mature into young men and women of God. These young men and women of God will develop into mature men and women of God who will become spiritual parents.

When you have a church that understands its apostolic mission, you will see entire cities turned upside down. No longer will a select few minister with the Father's heart, but an entire movement will flow and operate under this mantle. When our sons and daughters come in contact with this anointing, the restoration will be complete and the stage will be set for the greatest outpouring this world has ever known.

Only the Beginning

I was on cloud nine after experiencing so much from God in Brazil. Little did I understand that this was actually a new beginning in my life. God had so much more in store. One particular Sunday, after a glorious morning worship service in Lambertville, I returned to my office where I was pleasantly greeted by one of the couples in my congregation. After shaking hands, they began to share a burden they felt the Holy Spirit had placed on their hearts. "Pastor Craig, God has been telling us over and over again to pay your hotel, food, and registration for a pastor's conference being held in Toronto, Canada, this January."

The instant they spoke those words, I had a release from God and a burning desire in my spirit to go, so I accepted their offer and thanked them for their generosity. After the unique way in which God had ministered to me in Brazil, I was not about to try to figure things out when it came to the plans and purposes of God. Often, it's our minds that get us into trouble when it comes to faith and obedience.

While making preparations for the trip, another sister in the church contacted me and said, "Pastor, I heard about the conference you will be attending and the Holy Spirit has instructed me to pay the round-trip airfare on your behalf." What a blessing! After expecting to drive nine hours through the snow and ice of New England and Canada, I would be able to reach my destination in just 90 minutes instead. Praise God! To top it all off, another brother in the church blessed me with spending money. This was an all-expenses-paid trip, courtesy of the Father Himself. One thing is for sure, when God wants to accomplish something, money is never an issue. There was no doubt in my mind that a divine appointment was waiting at this conference.

Meeting the Father

The day came for my departure, and I was up and out of the house by 6:30 AM. After arriving at the airport, I checked my bags and then headed towards the proper gate and waited to board the plane. While sitting there, I decided to make good use of the time, so I opened my Bible to enjoy some additional reading.

Whenever reading scripture, I always follow a systematic approach, reading a minimum of one chapter a day from both the Old and New Testaments. This enables me to go through the entire Bible time and time again. When I opened my Bible to the next scheduled Old Testament reading, the text was Isaiah 55. The first word I saw was, "Ho!" This may seem insignificant, but I soon discovered how important this Scripture and the word "ho" would be to me. In fact, this verse would serve as the entry ticket of trust into an arena of ministry that was completely new for me.

After reading and meditating on this verse, I was interrupted by the flight attendant's announcement to begin boarding the jetliner. I placed my Bible back in my briefcase and followed the crowd onto the plane. After taking my assigned seat, I began to pray. While worshipping the Lord in this way, I looked at the vacant seat next to me and was suddenly overwhelmed with a sense that Jesus was present there!

As I continued to pray and worship, this realization stimulated a heart of thanksgiving. I thought back on how the Lord provided the finances that enabled me to go. As I continued to worship, I asked the Lord, "Why are you taking me to this pastors' conference?"

It was at that moment Jesus spoke the following words to my spirit, "I'm taking you to meet My Father." This was an overwhelming statement from the Lord, and the tears increased as I considered His words over and over again. I noticed a gentleman across the aisle watching me. The Holy Spirit had gotten His attention. When our eyes made contact, he asked me why I was going to Toronto. I explained to him I was a minister and would be attending a pastors' conference. When he learned that I was a pastor, he began to open his heart by asking many questions about faith and spirituality out of an obvious deep hunger. I could tell he was hanging onto every word I spoke, so we continued to share back and forth until our flight landed. As we were leaving the plane, I quietly prayed that this gentleman would come to know the Father as I was about to do.

After going through immigration, I collected my luggage, caught a taxi, and headed for the hotel. A blizzard had hit the area, leaving several feet of the white stuff everywhere. Finally I arrived at the hotel and checked into my room. I was eager to go to the church where the conference was being held because so much had been said about this ministry. I was now ready to experience everything firsthand. I boarded a shuttle bus and followed the crowd to the worship center. The instant I walked into the lobby of the church, I started to cry because the presence of God was so strong!

I knew I was where God wanted me to be. The moment I entered the sanctuary, I felt light-headed. I had not heard a single sermon or responded to one altar call, but I was already experiencing God's wonderful presence! I thought, *If I'm being affected like this already, I can't imagine what I'll be like after four days of ministry here.* Little did I know how true that statement would prove to be.

I quickly found a seat and began to drink from the river of God that was flowing around me. While I was enjoying the preaching, I was suddenly distracted by a shout that came from three rows in front of me. I couldn't believe my ears. Then it happened again. This time the shout came from behind me. It was as if a chain reaction began to take place.

All over the auditorium people were responding to the presence of God with the same shout. It was the word "Ho"—the same word I had read from Isaiah earlier, and it was coming from the mouths of Christians all over the auditorium. I was overwhelmed by God's love. He had taken the time to orchestrate all the details of my life, including my devotional reading, in order to prepare me for this conference. Even a simple word like "Ho" was important to my heavenly Father because He knew it would be important to me.

Through the years I have seen many things happen when the Holy Spirit enters a gathering of believers. Some people will fall, others will laugh, some will shake, shout or even run and dance, but I usually cry. This happens because something so deep within me rises up and possesses my entire being. I believe it's what David describes when he says in Psalms 42:7, "Deep calls unto deep at the noise of your waterfall."

As I sat there, it was as if a wave had hit me, and I fell to the floor. I was being baptized in the glory of God. At that same time I heard myself shouting with those around me. "Ho" came out of my vocal chords like a lightning bolt. Then it happened again and again, and I loved it! People looked at me and I looked at them. "Ho!" There it was again.

Before I knew it, the speaker had finished and the altars were now open for ministry. I didn't hesitate to respond. In fact, I ran to the front, fell on my face, and cried out to God for more. The Holy Spirit was invading me, and this was one invasion I didn't want to interfere with. Whatever God was doing on the inside of me, I was in complete agreement with it. It felt so good! When I finally got up from the floor, I realized I had been lying there for over an hour. It was a wonderful first day of the conference, and the great thing was that there were still had three days remaining.

"More, Lord, More!"

The next morning I arrived early. The featured speaker was Frank Houston, the former Assistant General Superintendent for the Assemblies of God in Australia and father to Pastor Brian Houston, who pastors Hillsong Christian Life Center in Sydney, Australia, where many wonderful praise and worship songs, such as "Shout to the Lord" have originated. I was excited to hear what this man of God had to say. Following a time of worship, the conference host introduced the speaker and the momentum began to build. Frank Houston is a small man in stature, but his preaching is as bold as a lion. I would liken him to an explosion looking for a place to happen. From the moment he began to speak, the audience was captivated. What a powerhouse he is! It was as if he had known who was coming and then had prepared his message with those individuals in mind. On that particular morning, he felt led to share the story of how he had been baptized in "The River." I wanted what he had and the wonderful thing is, God wanted it for me too.

Frank told how, for three days, he rolled from one end of his hotel room to the other, as he was being baptized in the river of God's glory. The glory was so strong that he couldn't stop rolling! This man was over 70 years old when this happened, and he explained how, in all of his years of ministry, he had never experienced a touch from God like the one he was describing to us.

He is a seasoned pastor who has moved in signs and wonders, and yet God had more for him. Jesus said, "Blessed are those who hunger and thirst for righteousness, for they shall be filled" (Matt. 5:6). I was hungry and thirsty and like all those around me, I was crying out for more. "More Lord, more!" was our common cry. When the altar call was given, I was the first one at the front.

I am a firm believer in ministry at the altar. I believe something special happens when people humble themselves in a corporate setting. In a way, it is similar to the cleansing process of a baking pan. After removing any excess food and debris, there is still a layer of burnt or crusted sections stuck to the pan. Once the pan has cooled down, these burnt or crusted areas become even harder and seem almost impossible to remove. When this happens, the only way to clean the pan properly is to allow it to soak in soap and hot water. After a time of soaking, the debris comes off and the pan looks like new again. All of us, in the course of living our daily lives, manage to collect some spiritual dirt and debris. When we learn to soak in the river of God, we are cleansed from hurts and sins that have held us back from being the vessel God has called us to be.

When I was lying prostrate at the altar that evening, God began to flood my innermost being. When I attempted to lift my head, I saw Frank Houston approaching me and heard him praying that the Father would penetrate me with His glory. When he uttered those words, I felt more love than I had ever felt in my life. It was such an overwhelming encounter with God. All I was able to do in response was to cry a fountain of tears. Something had pierced me deeply, and I would not be fully aware of what it was until the Saturday morning before my departure.

Meeting God

This conference was unlike any other pastor's conference I had attended because it wasn't about methods, it was about meeting God. Don't get me wrong, I believe there is a plan for ministry, but that plan comes from God, not from men. We can glean from other ministries, but just because something works for someone else doesn't necessarily mean it will work for you or me. We must never run with another person's vision; instead, we need to let God give us our own vision. Proverbs 29:18 states, "Where there is no vision, the people perish." The word translated here as "vision" from the Hebrew language can also be defined as "divine communication."

When we take the time to meet with God, He will give us the strategy He has ordained to reach the communities, cities, and nations where we live. Like Moses, I had been to the mountain, but now there was still one thing left for me to hear before returning to New Jersey.

Very early Saturday morning, just as I was waking up from a sound sleep, the presence of God filled my hotel room, stimulating a spirit of praise and worship within me. As I continued to worship, the glory increased, and an overwhelming sense of God's love permeated my room. It was at that moment when something happened to me that I never experienced before. As I lay there alone on the bed, a voice spoke to me. There was no mistaking it; I was hearing an audible voice. Whether it was the voice of Jesus or the voice of an angel, I'm not sure, but I am certain of one thing—heaven was its source.

Up to this point in my life, I had heard about men and women who had heard the audible voice of God, but I never thought it would happen to me. The words God communicated were simple and direct. He plainly said, "Now you have the Father's heart." The instant I heard that sentence, it was as if an arrow went through the center of my being. The only way to explain it is that I felt as if my heart was being pumped up like a hot water bottle. It continued to expand until I thought I would literally explode. A new capacity for love was being imparted to me beyond anything I had ever experienced. It was at this point that I remembered what Jesus spoke to my heart on the jetliner. When I had asked Him why He was taking me to Toronto, He had responded, "I'm taking you to meet My Father." Now it had happened! I met God the Father in a way I had never known Him before.

Since that day I have never been the same. God the Father came and opened me up and poured His heart into mine. As a result of this divine encounter, I have found a greater revelation of His plans and purposes.

God has literally turned my life upside down and the good news is that He desires this same kind of oneness with everyone. Many of us have stopped at the doorway, but now it's time to enter into His presence. The anointing is wonderful, but it is only the doorway to our final destination, His manifest presence—the glory of God! The Holy Spirit is calling us. He is saying, "Ho! Everyone who thirsts come to the waters" (Is. 55:1).

CHAPTER EIGHT

The Glory of the Father

For the earth will be filled with the knowledge of the glory of the Lord, as the waters cover the sea (Habakkuk 2:14).

An Outpouring of Glory

As we examine the glory of the Father, there is a key principle we need to understand in order to embrace the full impact of what is in store, not only for the church, but for the unsaved as well. An outpouring of glory from the Father's throne is about to baptize all the nations of the earth. What we are about to experience will be unlike any other revival that has graced the earth. This outpouring will be the capstone that pulls all past moves of God together. It will set the stage for a display of His manifest presence that will gain the attention of entire cities, regions, and nations. Jesus said the Church would do greater things than He did, and yet we struggle to share our faith on the job, pray before a meal, pay our tithes, or even get along with one another in the Body of Christ. Jesus is not going to return for a weak and self-centered church. When this wave of glory hits, it will transform the hearts of God's people.

There have been many moves of God throughout the centuries, but never an outpouring with the emphasis I am about to share with you. The revival I believe God has saved for last is going to center-around a "Revelation of God the Father." Let's examine the various moves of God throughout history to see what the emphasis has been.

The Day of Pentecost

On the day of Pentecost, this move of God gave birth to the Church, but it also brought with it a "Revelation of the Holy Spirit." Men and women alike received a mighty baptism in the Spirit, which provided a place of habitation for God, enabling each disciple to draw upon and operate in the same power that Jesus did during His earthly walk. Throughout this period in church history, great exploits were accomplished, the church advanced with unquenchable boldness in the face of much adversity, and the New Testament was written by the Apostles. This wave of Pentecost ran hard and long, spreading the message of the Gospel, but as is true of every wave, it eventually lost its momentum.

After Constantine received a vision from God of a flaming cross, he converted to Christianity as a young soldier. Following the death of his father in 309 AD, Constantine was later elevated to the position of Caesar, and with his newfound authority, he decreed Christianity to be the official religion of the State. Many would say, "What a miracle! God changed the course of an entire nation." This is true, but it is equally true that many who had been avid followers of Roman paganism converted to Christianity out of legal obligation, rather than out of Holy Spirit conviction. In other words, every Roman citizen was now considered a Christian, whether they liked it or not. History records that the same priests who ministered in the pagan temples of Rome were now appointed as leaders in the Church of Rome, bringing with them teaching contrary to the doctrine of the apostles, thus causing the church to develop into a highly political religious institution, void of any impact or fervor.

The Reformation

After the fall of the Roman Empire in 423 AD, the church entered into an era of history known as the Middle Ages or the Dark Ages, which describes the spiritual depravity prevalent throughout the nations. There was not much spiritual light or revelation during this 1000-year period. This absence of light brought an increase of darkness, witchcraft, immorality, and greed, which gained dominance in the political and religious arenas. Yes, there were spurts of isolated revival utilizing people such as Augustine, Boniface, Francis of Assisi, Peter Waldo, John Wycliffe, and John Huss, but nothing of a world magnitude. It wasn't until a Catholic monk by the name of Martin Luther came on the scene, that another move of God was released that would impact the four corners of the earth.

Historians named this revival "The Reformation." The effects of the Dark Ages had brought such decadence that an outpouring of God was necessary in order to reform the Church. The focus of this movement centered around a Revelation of Jesus, emphasizing God's grace, mercy, faith, and forgiveness of sins. Along with this message came great opposition because Luther's teachings were in direct conflict with the doctrines of the Catholic Church. Up until this point in time and history, there had not been a revival of this magnitude since the day of Pentecost.

The Great Awakening

The next outpouring from heaven that produced a world impact was "The Great Awakening," dating from the late 1600s into the early 1800s. Anointed preachers such as John and Charles Wesley, Jonathan Edwards, George Whitefield, Charles Finney and others were called into the ministry, proclaiming the message of salvation by grace and faith in Jesus Christ. Some historians have broken this movement into three revivals in one: "The First Great Awakening," "The English Great Awakening," and "The Second Great Awakening." Like "The Reformation," this movement centered around a revelation of Jesus.

The Pentecostal Movement

As time progressed into the late 1800s and early 1900s, all of the Church's attention was drawn to another worldwide move of God called "The Pentecostal Movement." This fresh outpouring of God's Spirit on Protestants and Catholics alike brought a new fire to the Church. The "Welsh Revival" came forth out of this movement and the "Azusa Street" outpouring exploded during this same period in a small dirt-floor facility in Los Angeles, California. Denominations like the Assemblies of God, Four Square, Church of God, and other independent groups evolved out of this revival. Like the day of Pentecost, this revival centered around a revelation of the Holy Spirit.

The Jesus Movement

In the 1960s another outpouring, which church historians named the "Jesus movement," made a worldwide impact when young men and women called hippies began filling churches. They traded in their drugs for Bibles and free love for God's love. These new converts were finding in Jesus what they had been searching for in their bizarre, yet sincere quests for truth. The freedom and spontaneity they enjoyed challenged religious leaders to rethink outdated methods of ministry. One major area of church life that would never be the same because of this new generation of believers would be its music. With this massive influx of people also came a new way to praise and worship God. The traditional hymn accompanied by the organ and piano was replaced with the modern four-piece rock band, consisting of a guitar, bass guitar, electric keyboards, and drums. This new style of church music was met with great opposition, but in spite of the protest, this fresh way of praising God continued to grow. It was during this revival that the singing of choruses and scripture songs became popular. Now some forty years later, this is the norm in churches, both Pentecostal and non-Pentecostal. The Jesus Movement, like the Reformation and the Great Awakening, centered-around a revelation of Jesus.

The Charismatic Movement

It seems once the turn of the twentieth century came, the waves of revival began to strike closer and closer in succession. The early 1900s brought the Pentecostal Movement; 1960 was the beginning of the Jesus Movement; and ten years later, 1970 would mark the start of yet another revival, the Charismatic Renewal. It was like the day of Pentecost all over again.

The boundary lines of doctrinal differences could not hold back this visitation from God. Catholic and Protestant believers alike were experiencing a fresh baptism of the Holy Spirit. Para-church organizations like the Full Gospel Businessmen's Fellowship and Women's Aglow grew during this time, tearing down the barriers of denominationalism and finding unity in the Spirit. Christian television took off during this decade of blessing, giving birth to and strengthening ministries that continue on to this day such as The 700 Club with Pat Robertson and TBN with Paul Crouch. Televangelists also experienced great prosperity during this era of blessing. Even Christian magazines and publishing companies were founded in order to keep up with the demand for Christian literature. Like prior movements, this revival centered around a revelation of the Holy Spirit.

The Word of Faith Movement

As time progressed, the church entered into the 1980s, and with this new decade came a new wind of revival. It was during this time the Word of Faith movement exploded. Preachers like Kenneth Hagin and Kenneth Copeland gained great visibility with this outpouring. What began as a simple message of faith and confession quickly grew into a worldwide movement. Churches calling themselves Word-of-Faith churches were pioneered in the United States and overseas. Bible colleges were established in order to train and send out leaders, citywide conferences were held, drawing thousands of people. International gatherings were sponsored, attracting leaders and believers from around the globe. God was accomplishing a specific purpose through the faith message.

This revival, like those of old, centered-around a revelation of Jesus, and because Jesus is the Word, this movement was God's way of bringing balance to the Church following the outpouring of the seventies. It is imperative for Christians to allow the Holy Spirit to have freedom, but never at the expense of violating the Word. The Word of Faith revival brought a blending of the Spirit and the Word, which would prepare the Church for what I believe will be the greatest move of all.

The Renewal Movement

When the Church entered into the decade of the 1990s, the wind of God began to blow again. The church had experienced great revivals through the centuries and yet there was still something lacking. A common cry began to rise before God's throne from God's people. Their prayer was, "More, Lord, more!" As the hunger continued to grow, so did a holy expectation.

Without warning, the Spirit of God began to fall on divinely chosen targets. In 1994 the Toronto Airport Vineyard Fellowship erupted in the Spirit, manifesting an abundance of joy in laughter, weeping, and various signs and wonders which became the norm in this once small, but now large congregation. People from around the world came to experience what was now known as "the Father's Blessing." As this renewal continued to grow, the focus on the first person of the trinity also grew.

One year later, on Father's Day, 1995, the church world's focus was then taken to Brownsville Assembly of God in Pensacola, Florida. The same glory that had transformed the Toronto church was now resting on this church in Florida. Do you think it was any coincidence that the Father's Blessing baptized Brownsville Assembly on Father's Day? God was speaking to His church.

If that were not enough, the fire continued to spread

into various parts of England, Australia, Africa, Europe, and even behind the Bamboo Curtain. Broken believers were being restored by this heavenly baptism of the Father's love. Books were now being written about the Father. National and international conferences were held emphasizing the first person of the Trinity. Songs of worship emphasizing the Father were written. Why was all of this attention being given to God the Father? This was God's way of balancing the scales. You see, the revivals of old were simply God's preparation. The Holy Spirit has been preparing mankind for what I believe will be the greatest revival ever to flood the earth.

Nothing But Dirt

The prophet Habakkuk prophesied regarding this end time event.

For the earth will be filled with the knowledge of the glory of the Lord, as the waters cover the sea (Hab. 2:14).

Considering this text, the first word I want to draw your attention to is "earth." God is promising that the "earth" will be filled. What does God mean when He says this? Why would He place His knowledge in soil, rocks and vegetation? The Hebrew word for earth used here is *erets*. It means, "land, earth, country, nations, world, people or inhabitants." It's the same word that is used in 2 Chronicles 7:14 when God proclaims,

If my people, which are called by My name, will humble themselves, and pray, and seek My face, and turn from

their wicked ways; then will I hear from heaven, and will forgive their sin, and will heal their land [erets].

Erets is also used in Isaiah 6:3 when the prophet says,

And one cried unto another, and said, "Holy, holy, holy, is the LORD of hosts: the whole earth {erets} is full of his glory."

There is that same word again. Why would God fill the earth with His glory? In answer to this question, reread these two verses with the definition of *erets* in mind. The latter part of 2 Chronicles 7:14 would read,

then will I hear from heaven, forgive their sin, and heal their erets [land, earth, country, nations, world, people or inhabitants].

God is not talking about healing a rock, purifying polluted waters, or cleaning up contaminated waste from a landfill. He is dealing with a spiritual healing of people. Forgiveness of sins and spiritual healing go hand in hand. This same principle applies at the closing of Isaiah 6:3, which reads, "the whole erets [land, earth, country, nations, world, people, or inhabitants] is full of His glory." Again, God is speaking about people.

In my travels, I have had the opportunity to observe many different types of soil compositions. I have seen yellow dirt, red clay, white sandy soil, and the rich dark brown dirt ideal for farming. Now think about that for a moment. Each of these soil compositions coincide with the major race colors of the earth. In Genesis 2:7 it says,

And the Lord God formed man of the dust (dirt) of the ground, and breathed into his nostrils the breath of life; and man became a living being.

Man was made from the dirt of the earth. Yes, there are varying shades of dirt, but the fact still remains that dirt is dirt. This is one of many reasons why I believe racism is such an inferior and unintelligent way of thinking. In essence, racism is declaring one shade of dirt better than another. If this were true, then that would mean red clay might be valued most because of the red brick fashioned from it or the dark rich soil because it is used for farming. One shade of dirt is not better than another and neither is one race superior over another. Every race and nation provides something unique that we can all benefit from because that is the way the Father designed it to be. Whether in food, technology, precious stones, oil reserves, or personal disciplines, every nation serves a purpose. When God looks at man He doesn't see their color, He only sees their specific purpose in His overall plan for mankind. We have all proceeded from one Father and are part of the same family.

When I look at the people of Asia, India, Africa, North America. South America, and Europe, I see yellow dirt, red dirt, black dirt, and white dirt. God prophesied through Isaiah that the entire earth (erets)—all nationalities—would be filled with the knowledge of His glory. The focus is not on geology, but on anthropology (the study of man), who was created in God's image.

Armed and Dangerous

The prophet then continues by saying the earth (people) will be "filled" with the knowledge of the glory of the Lord. I love this word "filled" in the Hebrew. Isaiah uses the word *male* {maw-lay}" in this Scripture, which is defined as, "filled to the full, overflowing, abounding, satisfied or armed." While researching this definition, I was especially drawn to the word "armed." It reminded me of the Wanted Posters from the Old West with pictures of outlaws like Jesse James and Billy the Kid printed on them. Underneath the picture, they would describe the crime for which they were guilty. Some would read, "Wanted dead or alive." Others described the outlaws as "Armed and dangerous." They were armed with weapons such as handguns or rifles and they were not only experienced in handling these weapons, but they were not afraid to use them. The thought of taking another life was no longer an issue to these men, and this is what made them so dangerous.

From a spiritual perspective, do we see ourselves as being armed and dangerous? Does Satan and his evil kingdom view us as a threat against the strongholds of hell? There are too many Christians who hold the devil's power in higher esteem than God's power. When a blood-washed, Holy-Spirit-filled believer walks into a demon-infested room, the devil and his spirits of darkness tremble in fear because of what we possess. Whether you know it or not, there is more power and authority in the weakest of all saints than Satan and his demons have combined together.

Yada

The prophet proclaims that the earth (people) will be filled (armed) with the "knowledge of the glory of the Lord." Notice the emphasis is on knowledge and not the glory. In the Hebrew the word used for knowledge is *yada* {yaw-dah}. There is an intimacy associated with this word that will help us understand what the Father wants us to draw from this portion of scripture. Genesis 4:1 reads,

Now Adam knew (yada) Eve his wife, and she conceived and bore Cain, and said, "I have acquired a man from the Lord."

The word "knew" in this verse is the past tense of the Hebrew word *yada*. Knowing is associated with conception and childbirth. By definition, *yada* means, "To know with certainty, intimate knowledge or intercourse," which reveals a physical union between a husband and a wife, and in this case, Adam and Eve. This word depicts the most intimate experience a man and a woman can share together—sexual intercourse. If we carry this definition over into Habakkuk 2:14, we would see that there is an intimacy of knowledge God wants His people filled (armed) with.

Daniel 11:32b states,

But the people who know their God shall be strong and carry out great exploits.

The word "strong" used here can also be defined as "restored." Notice in this verse how knowledge brings restoration. "The people who know their God shall be strong (restored)." Areas of our lives where we have experienced failure whether through bad decisions, unjust treatment, or simply the aftermath of spiritual warfare, are places where God has promised not only restoration (strength), but also great exploits—a demonstration of signs and wonders. If these great exploits are missing, then maybe the problem is a lack of knowledge.

Hosea 4:6 reads, "My people are destroyed for lack of knowledge." We again find the deciding factor between victory and defeat is knowledge. Even the Apostle Paul understood this principle when he wrote in Philippians 3:10,

That I may know Him and the power of His resurrection, and the fellowship of His sufferings, being conformed to his death.

As Christians, when we enter into an intimate knowledge or oneness of knowledge with the Father, then we will begin to comprehend and draw from His glory. The secret is not *getting more glory*, but *releasing the glory* that is already at our disposal. Paul also wrote in Colossians 2:9-10,

For in Him dwells all the fullness of the Godhead in bodily; and you are complete in Him who is the head of all principality and power.

This is the kind of knowledge Jesus operated in during His earthly walk. He would constantly draw from the Father's glory while ministering to the multitudes, or even to one individual at a time. When the Church enters into this same level of revelation, there will be no stopping her. Now Christians run from meeting to meeting, church to church, counselor to counselor, and prayer group to prayer group searching for more of God's glory. The truth of the matter is, the fullness of His glory is already within us. The key, then, is not getting more, but learning how to tap into and release this divine reservoir of the Father.

God's Reputation

Look at Habakkuk 2:14 with me again.

For the earth [people] will be filled [armed], with the knowledge [intimate revelation] of the glory of the Lord, as the waters cover the sea.

What is God's glory? Many times you'll hear people use the words "anointing" and "glory" interchangeably, but they are not one in the same. The Hebrew word for glory is *kabowd* [kaw-bodé]. Its definition is, "Glory, honor, abundance, riches, fame, splendor, and reputation." In other words, the glory is who God is.

Everyone has a reputation, whether it is good or bad. The way a reputation is established is by what someone has accomplished, the possessions they have acquired, and the character they manifest on a consistent basis. So, for those who have achieved greatness, obtained abundance of wealth, and display an impeccable character, they have established a good reputation for themselves. Their reputation is their glory.

God has a reputation as well. His reputation is His glory. When Moses received the call of God to lead the nation of Israel out of Egypt, he was concerned that the people would not follow him. Why? Moses didn't have a good reputation in Egypt because he was a known murderer who was exiled from that country. Who would listen to the instruction of a criminal? Therefore, when Moses asked, "Whom shall I say has sent me when I go to them?" God's response was, "Tell them I Am has sent you." God was trading the tarnished reputation (glory) of Moses for His own spotless reputation (glory). He was saying, "Moses you will not face the challenges of Egypt with your own abilities and resources, but with the ability and resource of My kingdom, the limitless power of My right hand, and the integrity of My Word. Whatever needs you experience, 'I AM' the one to meet those needs."

God wants us as believers to know there is nothing that goes beyond the influence of His glory. When His glory is revealed, sickness and disease must go, blinded eyes are opened, the lame are made to walk, the dead are brought back to life, sins are forgiven, and Satan and all demon spirits must release their captives because of who HE IS. In Hebrews 11:6 the writer states,

> *But without faith it is impossible to please Him, for he that comes to God must believe that HE IS* (NKJV).

Unfortunately, man wants his own glory (reputation) to fill the earth. Isn't that what happened with the tower of Babel? Genesis 11: 4 records,

> *And they said, "Come, let us build ourselves a city, and a tower whose top is in the heavens; let us make a name for ourselves lest we be scattered abroad over the face of the whole earth."*

The people of Babel were consumed with building a tower that would cause their name to be known throughout the land. Jesus had no interest in building His own reputation. In fact, Philippians 2:7 reads, "He made himself of no reputation." What does this tell us? Jesus came to do His Father's will, He came to speak His Father's words, and He came to display His Father's miraculous power through signs and wonders. Everything He did pointed to the Father.

The Apostle Paul says in 1 Corinthians 1:31, "Let him who glories, glory in the Lord." In other words, whose reputation or glory are we looking to further? I believe the reason we haven't seen the glory of God revealed to the extent He desires to display His manifest presence is because the Church has been too busy promoting their own ministries and agendas rather than the Father's. When we lay down our dreams, our wills, our hopes, and aspirations, then and only then, will we be able to partake of the glory He has prepared for us. In 1 Peter 5:1, Peter states, "We are partakers of His glory." It's not about establishing our reputations, it's about proclaiming God's glory (reputation) in everything we say, do, and think.

The Doorway to the Glory

Remember, at times people may use the words "anointing" and "glory" interchangeably, but they are not one in the same. Let me make the following distinctions between the two. The glory is God's reputation, whereas the anointing is the authority or legal right to access the glory. I'll explain it this way. In my travels abroad, I was required to obtain a legal passport in order to have access in and out of the United States. Just as this passport gives me the legal right to return to the nation of my physical birth, the anointing gives every believer the legal right to return to that heavenly place of their spiritual birth for shelter, protection, strength and whatever else may be needed in advancing the Father's will in our lives and in the lives of others. Without the anointing, there is no deliverance, no healing, no forgiveness, no restoration, or relationship because the anointing is the doorway of entrance into the Father's glory where our provision waits. That's the principle behind Philippians 4:19,

And my God [The Father] *shall supply all your need according to His riches in glory* [the Father's manifest presence] *by Christ Jesus* [the anointing].

Just as the glory belongs to the Father, the anointing belongs to the Son. Many fast and pray for the anointing of

God on their lives and ministries, and this is a good thing, but the anointing is not our final destination. It is the stepping stone of getting us to that place in the Spirit where the manifest presence or glory of the Father moves unhindered in restoring order where Satan has disrupted the perfect will of God.

When the Church embraces this *rhema* of the Father's glory and begins to access this spiritual dimension corporately, there is going to be an explosion in the heavenlies that will produce a holy tidal wave, ushering in with it millions upon millions of souls into the Father's kingdom. This spiritual phenomenon will restore the Church to that place God had always reserved for her and enable the Body of Christ to fulfill the Great Commission and hasten the return of the Lord.

This move of God is closer than you think. Are you ready? Do you anticipate this revival with joy and excitement, or do you dread an outpouring of this magnitude? The Father has set the wheels in motion and He wants you to be a part of the fulfillment of this divine prophecy. Cry out to God! Let Him hear the prayer of your heart. Ask Him to prepare and use you in this final harvest. Whether you're a backslider or perhaps you've never committed your life to the Lord, it's never too late to make things right with Him. All you have to do is confess your sin, become a disciple, and then wait on the Lord until He reveals your marching orders.

CHAPTER NINE

Answered Prayer

Then He said to His disciples, "The harvest truly is plentiful, but the laborers are few. Therefore pray the Lord of the harvest to send out laborers into His harvest" (Matt. 9:37-38).

Harvest Time

When Jesus spoke the above words to His disciples, His focus was not on the immediate harvest at hand, even though there was much to be gathered, but His attention was looking ahead to the end-time harvest that will sweep the entire earth. Even then, Jesus saw the magnitude of the revival that would precede His return. Just as the disciples did not fully comprehend His words, I believe the twenty-first century church has no idea what the Father is about to release, for if we did, we all would be working day and night to prepare for this great outpouring.

In the spring of 2001, the midwest region of the United States experienced devastating floods due to torrential rains and thawing snow. As the waters continued to rise in these small towns, people came out in advance to prepare for the flooding by filling sandbags and forming assembly lines in order to distribute and stack the bags. Residents moved furniture and other valuables to the second floors of their homes, while others transported items to a safer location. Rescue equipment was brought in and positioned at key locations in order to minimize travel time to the point of crisis. People stocked food and other non-perishables in preparation for the worst. Generators were purchased and configured to power entire houses in case of electrical outages. Firewood was acquired and stocked to provide heat during this time. Windows were taped and boarded for protection against the high winds and flying debris. In isolated areas, families were even evacuated because the threat was beyond human ability to safeguard. Why all of this preparation? Because the only way a flood of this magnitude could be managed is by advance planning and strategic positioning. This same principle applies in respect to the final outpouring the Father has promised to all peoples.

God Will Not Send Anything We Are Not Equipped To Handle

The Church talks about, sings of, and holds prayer meetings crying out for God to send a revival. Special campaigns are sponsored in hopes of igniting the fire of God, but the bottom line is, do we have a work force in place that can host the greatest revival ever to sweep the entire face of the earth? God will not send what we are not equipped to handle. Before we ask the Father for revival, like Jesus, we first need to petition Him for laborers, and that is the point at which the Church now is in Bible history. The prayer Jesus prayed and commanded us to pray in Matthew 9:37-38 is about to be answered. A heavenly work force of great magnitude is about to be placed in position.

The First Wave

A few years ago I enjoyed a week of powerful ministry in the nation of Singapore. The people there were some of the most gracious, as well as spiritually hungry, people I had ever encountered. After returning, I remember in particular the first service held in my home church. My message that day was challenging and the ministry around the altar was rich and sweet. There was an unusual stirring in the hearts of the congregation. People were on the floor weeping, laughing, shaking, repenting, and praising God.

Then in the midst of this divine visitation, the Lord opened my spiritual eyes, and as I gazed toward heaven, I saw a wave coming in the distance. At first, it was difficult to judge its size because it was so far away, but the closer it got, the bigger it became until I realized this was no ordinary wave, but a tidal wave. It was larger than any manmade or natural structure on the face of the earth. In the midst of this vision, a holy awe came over me. Instead of running *away* from the wave in fear for my life, I began to run *towards* it. The instant I did so, the wave hit me, causing the power of God to flow through me like a mighty rushing river. When this happened, I was knocked to the floor. While laying there trembling beneath the mantle of His glory, the Lord revealed the interpretation of this vision.

At that moment, He spoke the following words: "This is the first of two waves which I will send on the earth. They will not be as past waves, for these waves are end-time waves. The first wave will bring with it 'the prodigals.' For these men and women both young and old once served me, but then lost heart. This wave will turn their hearts back to Me. They will return with a love and dedication that will not lose heart. Love them, embrace them, restore them, and commission them, for without them you cannot be a part of the end-time revival. Without them, My church will not have the workforce in place to oversee the great harvest that is about to come. Only those who embrace My first wave will experience the full blessing of My second wave."

What a powerful word! From the time the Holy Spirit birthed this word in my spirit, God began to reveal a series of biblical examples that support this prophecy in principle, as well as authenticity.

Prodigals in the Enemy's Camp

First Samuel 13:16-23 records how the Philistines had crippled the Jewish nation by passing a decree which forbade the profession of the blacksmith throughout all the land of Israel. The Philistine army did this in order to weaken the armies of Israel because the absence of a blacksmith meant the absence of swords, spears, and other instruments of war. Murderous threats and vandalism by the Philistine raiders were responsible for running off all the blacksmiths, which left Israel defensively and offensively vulnerable. When you combine this with the size of the Philistine army surrounding Saul and Israel, which numbered 30,000 chariots, 6,000 horsemen, and foot soldiers as many as the sand on the seashore, discouragement was at an all-time high. Fear began to dominate the Israelites, causing many soldiers to lose heart and desert, leaving Saul and Jonathan with only 600 warriors and two swords. This was not a good morale builder at all.

In the midst of this dilemma, is a king and a prince—father and son—both carrying the same blood, but spiritually not the same. Even though Jonathan was the son of Saul, his heart was entirely different from the heart of his father. Saul was a man who was ruled by his feelings and fears, whereas Jonathan was a man of faith. Saul wanted a guarantee of victory before fighting, but Jonathan acted in order to guarantee victory. Therefore, Saul and the armies of Israel remained in hiding.

Things could not continue this way much longer. If Saul, Jonathan, and the 600 remaining soldiers were going to get out of there alive, then something needed to happen! First Samuel 14:1 says,

> *Now it happened one day that Jonathon the son of Saul said to the young man who bore his armor, "Come let us go over to the Philistines' garrison that is on the other side." But he did not tell his father.*

It was quite obvious that a substantial amount of time had lapsed since the Philistines' had made their threats and still Saul did nothing in retaliation. I believe the spiritual inconsistency Jonathan observed in his father's roller-coaster life, played a major role in developing the strong commitment Jonathan now had in God. Saul was everything Jonathan desired not to be. Finally, one morning, Jonathan couldn't take it any longer and couldn't stomach the disgrace God's name was experiencing because of Saul's lack of faith, so he said to his armor bearer in 1 Samuel 14:1, "Come, let us go over to the Philistines' garrison that is on the other side." Once they arrived at the base of the camp, Jonathan said to his armor bearer,

Very well, let us cross over to these men, and we will show ourselves to them. If they say thus to us, "Wait until we come to you," then we will stand in our place and not go up to them. But if they say thus, "Come up to us." Then we will go up. For the Lord has delivered them into our hand, and this will be a sign to us (1 Sam. 14:8-10).

Jonathan was ready for battle! He was tired of the lies, pagan ways, and intimidations of the Philistines, and it wouldn't take much now to convince him to fight. Here he is seen standing before this Philistine stronghold with only his armor-bearer and one sword. At this point Jonathan tells his armor bearer, "If they say thus, 'Come up to us.' This will be a sign to us." Now I don't know about you, but if I had thousands of enemy soldiers standing before me, I could think of a dozen better signs then than, "If they tell us to come up." I would ask that an elephant would run by singing the chorus, "Shout to the Lord." I would request that the sky would grow dark and hailstones of fire would begin to fall from the heavens. If I were Jonathan, I would have petitioned for something very definite and supernatural, not "If they say come up to us, this will be a sign."

Sure enough, when Jonathan and his armor bearer finished climbing up to the Philistine garrison, it happened just as God had purposed in Jonathan's heart. One by one, the enemy soldiers began to fall in defeat at Jonathan's feet. After the first one fell, the armor bearer picked up the wounded Philistines' sword and killed him. As these two Hebrews continued to fight, an anointing came over them, which threw the enemy's entire camp into confusion. Like Samson, when he ripped apart a lion with his bare hands and like the prophet Elijah, who, after prophesying the rains were coming had the ability to outrun the chariots of Ahab,

Jonathan and his armor bearer fought with supernatural strength and precision.

After only a short period of time, Jonathan and his armor bearer were able to defeat nearly 20 Philistine soldiers and set the rest of the Philistine camp into utter confusion. Meanwhile, Saul found out about the situation through his watchmen back in his own camp. As the Philistine army melted away, a metamorphosis began to take place. Some Jewish soldiers, who had become disgruntled fighting for Saul and Israel, now served as mercenaries for the cause of the Philistine nation. While Jonathan and his armor bearer continued to forge ahead, I believe the hearts of these Israelite mercenaries were pierced when they looked into the eyes of two men who were willing to lay down their lives for the God they loved so passionately. Their inspiration was the spark that God used to bring about the transformation of these misguided Hebrews. The hearts of these wayward soldiers were turned back to God, thus providing Jonathan with skilled soldiers equipped with the finest weaponry available. What a divine act of wisdom! God knew all along this day would come and He strategically planted prodigals in the enemy's camp, soldiers who would rise up on behalf of Israel when they were needed most.

The impact of this attack was so intense that confusion began to sweep through the ranks, causing Philistine to fight against Philistine. The noise from the battle increased to such a level that Saul and his troops heard the sound from where they were camped. At that moment, courage rose in their hearts and they came to the assistance of Jonathan and his armor bearer by entering into the battle with them. Victory was so strong you could smell it in the air. Even the men of Israel, who had run in fear and were hiding in the mountains, came out and joined in the battle.

All of these fearful military backsliders experienced a change of heart because of Jonathan's faith and obedience. What began as an impossible situation for 600 Jewish soldiers possessing two swords, turned into a miracle of God because of one man's faith. There was no time to recruit and train new soldiers because the heat of the battle demanded more troops immediately. From a human perspective there was no remedy, but from God's view everything was in place. These backslidden turncoats, who had pledged allegiance to the Philistine army, experienced a change of heart in simply a moment.

The Sleeping Giant

I believe this same phenomenon will transpire spiritually before God uses His Church to gather in the final harvest of souls. There is a revival coming that is bigger than any move of God in past history. This harvest of souls is going to require every hand on deck. The church, in its current condition, cannot handle a move of this magnitude, but with the assistance of restored prodigals, we will have a workforce or an army in place capable of establishing God's kingdom worldwide.

The Holy Spirit is about to resurrect "the sleeping giant." There are backslidden and burned out preachers, teachers, evangelists, worship leaders, musicians, youth workers, children's ministers, successful businessmen with administrative gifts and committed men and women with help gifts, who, like the Israelite mercenaries, are about to experience a change of heart. These prodigals, like Samson, will be restored in worship and in ministry. They will be different! Like the prodigal son, they will return humble and broken. The only expectation they will have will be serve the

One who gave them a second chance. Scripture states in Luke 7:47,

> *Therefore I say unto you, her sins, which are many, are forgiven, for she loved much. But to whom little is forgiven, the same loves little.*

The greater the grace, the greater the gratitude. For example, it wasn't until after Lazarus was resurrected from the dead and given a second chance at life that he stood for anything spiritually. Prior to his resurrection miracle, the emphasis was always on the dedication and loyalty of his sisters, Mary and Martha, but after Jesus called him back from the grave, his life and testimony made such an impact that the Pharisees sought to have him killed. A resurrected prodigal will accomplish great things.

The fields are ready for harvest, but there is a shortage of laborers. Like Ezekiel, we need to prophesy over the valley of dry bones. There is a workforce of laborers God is calling back to life. A great multitude of soldiers is about to be raised up. Yes they have made mistakes, but God sees and has the ability to change the hearts of the most severe backsliders. The Holy Spirit will change the hearts of these prodigals from a heart of stone into a heart of flesh. Like the woman caught in the act of adultery, the words of Jesus will echo in their hearts and mind, "Go and sin no more." They will appreciate their forgiveness and restoration and totally forsake the sin that once bound them. The hour is close and the clock is winding down. Time is so short you can almost hear the rattling of the dry bones. Let's not miss the day of visitation. If we choose to embrace a spirit of unforgiveness and rejection, like the older brother did in the parable of the prodigal son, then we will miss the Church's greatest hour of visitation. Only those who embrace this first wave of restoration will have the necessary work force in place to handle the magnitude of the second wave that will usher in with it the greatest harvest of souls the world has ever known.

CHAPTER TEN

The Greatest Awakening

And this gospel of the kingdom will be preached in all the world as a witness to all the nations, and then the end will come (Matthew 24:14).

Confirmation

Around 10:30 PM, I was working swiftly to finish packing for two overseas events in which I was scheduled to speak—a crusade in Western Australia and a pastor's conference in Eastern Australia. There was an excitement in my spirit regarding this trip.

God came to me in a dream a number of years ago and revealed that one day He would open the door for me to preach alongside many great men and women of God. The night this happened, I was alone in the church sanctuary worshipping and interceding before the Lord. I must have continued this way for several hours when, at some point, I fell asleep. It was at that moment the Lord allowed me to see myself standing and ministering with many great men and women of God. There were many giants of the faith represented, as well as faces I didn't recognize. I knew the unfamiliar faces were people like myself that the Lord was about to resurrect in ministry. It was an overwhelming vision. The next thing I recall is waking up with tears streaming down my cheeks.

As I do with every vision or dream, I tucked it away in my heart, and knew that, if indeed this was from God, He would bring it to pass. Since that night, I have checked many names off my list from that vision of those with whom I ministered, and now I was about to remove one more. Dr. David Yonggi Cho, Pastor of the World's largest church in Seoul, Korea, was one of the four featured speakers I was scheduled to minister with in Australia. He was one of the many faces I saw in my dream and now divine providence had opened the door to share the message of the "Father's Heart" alongside this giant in the faith.

As I continued to pack for my trip, I kept telling myself, "Concentrate, concentrate, concentrate, Craig, so you don't forget anything." There's nothing worse than getting halfway around the world and then realizing you forgot to bring something of importance. In the midst of all this rushing around, I added to the confusion by turning the television on. I was pleased to discover that "The 700 Club" was on, so I proceeded to shine my shoes while listening to the show. The next guest Pat Robertson was about to speak with was Steve Hill, the evangelist God used to usher in the revival that impacted Pensacola, Florida. When the interview began, the topic of revival was its immediate focus. Pat and Steve began talking about the thousands of salvations that had resulted from this sovereign outpouring from heaven. It was at that moment the Holy Spirit got my undivided attention, because I heard Steve begin to define the next move the Holy Spirit told him would sweep the earth.

He said, "The Lord told me this would not be a Great Awakening, for this will be greater than any awakening of the past. I have called this next revival the GREATEST AWAKENING, for this outpouring will bring in the end-time harvest prior to My return."

When he spoke those words, I jumped up and began to shout and worship the Lord. For only two days before hearing Steve Hill speak this prophetic word, God had come to me while I was praying and had spoken the same message to me. The Holy Spirit said to me, "I have given a name to the next revival. Some will say this is another Great Awakening, but that is not the name I have given it. I have called this next move THE GREATEST AWAKENING. I have called it the greatest because it will bring in the greatest harvest of souls the world has ever known. Never before and never again will there be a visitation like it. Along with this harvest will also come great signs and wonders, for this outpouring will reveal My glory to all the nations. The whole earth will know that there is no one like Me." After He spoke these words to me originally, I was trembling and now after hearing them confirmed through Steve Hill, I was once again trembling.

Noah's Faith

In previous chapters, I shared with you how I believe the Scriptures teach a revival greater than any other revival known to history is about to be released from heaven. We looked at how there were revivals that focused on Jesus or the Holy Spirit, but never was there a revival centered around a revelation of the first person of the Trinity, God the Father. As I began to pray over and research this truth, I found there were key references in the Word that brought greater clarification as well as confirmation to this end-time event.

In Genesis 6: 5-6 we find the world had become such a wicked place, that God was sorry He had created man.

Then the Lord saw that the wickedness of man was great in the earth, and that every intent of the thoughts of his heart was only evil continually. And the Lord was sorry that He had made man on the earth, and He was grieved in His heart.

At this point Noah came to the forefront as someone who had grace in the eyes of the Lord. Genesis 6:8 states, "But Noah found grace in the eyes of the Lord." God saw that there was something in the heart of Noah that could be trusted with such a monumental task as building the ark.

What God commanded Noah to do made no sense, from a human perspective. There was no record in history that the earth had ever experienced a flood of water. In fact, up to this point in time and history, there was no such thing as rain. Scripture records in Genesis 2:5-6 that,

God had not caused it to rain on the earth and there was no man to till the ground; but a midst went up from the earth and watered the whole face of the ground.

God revealed to Noah that an act of nature, which had never transpired throughout the entire course of history, was about to happen. How would you or I have responded if

God spoke the following to us? "Because of the wickedness in the hearts and thoughts of mankind, rain is going to fall from the heavens and cause the entire face of the earth to be flooded with water. These floodwaters will destroy every living thing on the face of the earth. I will build a new generation of men and women from your offspring and from the offspring of animal life I will preserve with you. My plan of preservation is that you construct an ark according to the specifications I reveal to you. When it is completed, I will bring the animals two by two to the ark and then you and your family will board last. After this, I will close the ark door and the rains will begin." Can you imagine having God come to you and speak those words? Noah not only believed the word of the Lord, but he acted on it by constructing the ark according to every detail God gave him. Noah was a man of faith.

Understanding Typology

As I began to ponder and study this portion of Scripture, God revealed to me some awesome prophetic revelations regarding this historical event. Throughout the Word of God you will find what Bible scholars call typologies. Typologies are events and or individuals that convey one truth, but symbolize another meaning as well. One example of this is Jonah. In the book of Jonah there is a prophet of God who is directed by the Holy Spirit to go and preach the Word of the Lord to a City called Nineveh. When the prophet received his orders, he was outraged. He didn't feel these people deserved an opportunity to repent of their sins, so he sought to run from God's presence by boarding a ship headed towards a different City called Tarshish. In the midst of his disobedience, God sent a storm in order to get Jonah's attention. As the sailors attempted to settle the ship in the storm, they found their efforts were to no avail. Finally, after realizing that his own disobedience was the reason the storm had gained such momentum, Jonah informed the crew that the only way to calm the storm would be to throw him overboard into the sea. At first the sailors all refused, but finally, in fear for their lives, they cast him into the raging waters. At this point, God sent a large fish to swallow the prophet. Over the next three days, while in the belly of this huge fish, God changed his heart from one of rebellion to one of obedience.

The next time you hear Jonah's name mentioned is by Jesus in Matthew 12:39-40,

> *But He answered and said to them, "An evil and adulterous generation seeks after a sign, and no sign will be given to it except the sign the prophet Jonah. For as Jonah was three days and three nights in the belly of the great fish, so will the Son of Man be three days and three nights in the heart of the earth."*

Jesus addressed the demands of the religious leaders who wanted a sign that He indeed was the Messiah the Jewish people had been awaiting. Jesus uses the prophet's deliverance from the great fish as a typology of His own resurrection from the dead that would transpire after His crucifixion.

The Mini-Earth

As we consider the Noah account, there is a typology found in this story directly related to the end-time outpouring that is coming just prior to the Lord's return, and which will bring the end-time harvest or "The Greatest Awakening." Take a moment to look again at Noah and the ark. Once the floodwaters came, the ark became a temporary dwelling place, or "mini-earth," providing protection, provision, and a procreation environment for all remaining living things. The length of time spent on the ark would be determined by the amount of time it took for the waters to subside. In God's eyes, the ark was only meant to be a temporary dwelling, not a permanent one.

Think about this for a moment. Where has God ordained for His saints to spend eternity—in heaven or on earth? According to Scripture, the answer is heaven. Jesus said in John 14:2-3,

> *In My Father's house are many mansions; if it were not so, I would have told. I go to prepare a place for you. And if I go and prepare a place for you, I will come again and receive you to Myself; that where I am, there you may be also.*

Just as God never intended Noah, his family, and the remaining living things of creation to remain in the ark, God never intended the earth to be man's permanent dwelling place either. Once we grasp this important principle, we can continue to discover the many prophetic revelations within the Noah account.

The Wait

One of the hardest things for a follower of God to do is to wait. Everything is exciting when the Holy Spirit first unfolds His plan, but then comes the dreaded part He saves until later. God waits until we have ventured so deep into His plan that there's no turning back, and then it's at this point that He lets us know there will be a season of waiting involved before the blessing unfolds. Think of all the times when God has spoken a prophetic word over you. Little did you know all the time and breaking that would be involved before that word could be fulfilled in your life.

A nugget of truth to remember during those waiting periods is that God is not moved by time, but God moves time. For example, God caused time to stand still in Joshua 10:13 when Joshua and the Israelites were battling on behalf of Gibeon's safety. And that's why Moses was able to see back to the very beginning and record the creation account in the Book of Genesis. It is also why John the Apostle was supernaturally transported to the end of time for the purpose of recording end-time events leading up to the Lord's return. Again, God doesn't answer to time, time answers to God. After receiving God's directive, it took Noah 120 years to complete the construction of the ark. It's never recorded once during this waiting period that he ever complained or took matters into his own hands. He was ridiculed by the multitudes, but he maintained his vision and direction. He was a man who lived up to his name.

The name Noah means, "Rest." If given the task this man was given, most people would be stressed and heavily medicated in order to survive from day to day. But this wasn't the case with Noah. In Hebrews 4:9-10 the author says,

There remains therefore a rest for the people of God. For he who has entered His rest has himself also ceased from his works as God did from His.

Noah is a type of God the Father. Not only does his name reflect this, but the responsibilities he was given are a depiction of it as well. After the flood had eliminated all forms of life on the earth, He was left with the awesome task of overseeing the repopulation of the earth. Just as this mantle had once covered the shoulders of Adam, it had now been placed upon Noah. It's very important to understand this, or we will miss a powerful insight God the Father wants us to comprehend in order to properly prepare for the end-time harvest the Holy Spirit has called, "The Greatest Awakening."

The Flesh Eater

As the waters began to subside, we see in Genesis 8:6-7 that Noah took a raven and released it in order to see how much longer their stay in the ark would be.

> *So it came to pass, at the end of forty days, that Noah opened the window of the ark which he had made. Then he sent out a raven, which kept going to and fro until the waters had dried up from the earth.*

What was Noah doing here? God was illustrating through this action a far greater message that really had nothing to do with the water outside their dwelling place. If you were to research the definition of a raven, you would find it's nothing more than a common crow that feeds on the dead flesh of a decaying carcass. In other words, a raven is a flesh eater.

A couple years ago, I remember getting into my car and heading for one of the area's Christian universities where I was scheduled to speak for the morning chapel service. As I was traveling on the Pennsylvania Turnpike, I couldn't help but notice three or four large crows in the middle of the road. Cars were swerving in order to miss the birds, and yet they seemed oblivious to the danger of the moving vehicles. When my car was just about at the location where the crows had gathered, I switched lanes in order to better see what these birds were so drawn to. When I passed by, I was astounded to see the flattened carcass of a small animal such as a squirrel or rabbit. These crows were risking their lives to eat the remaining flesh of a two- or three-day-old road kill. These birds were so driven to satisfy their craving for flesh that they were willing to lay down their very lives to get it. This is the exact same species of bird that Noah first released from the ark window in an attempt to answer the question that was on everyone's mind, "How much longer until we leave this place?" When it was all said and done, what answer did this raven's release bring? This raven did what all ravens do. The bird continued to fly in order to satisfy its craving for more flesh and the end result was it never returned. What does this tell us?

The raven is a typology of our human flesh. Just as our flesh is driven to satisfy its earthly appetites, the raven in our text was driven to find and devour more flesh. That's right, after its release, the raven was not in search of dry land, but rather it was looking for more flesh to eat. That raven could have cared less about the desires of Noah, just as our flesh could care less about the desires of God. Like our flesh, the raven's motives were self-centered and self-satisfying. The promises of God will never be obtained through the resources of the flesh. Just as lions beget lions, whales beget whales, and eagles beget eagles, flesh begets flesh.

The way we begin is so important. When you start right, the foundation is there to finish right, but if you start wrong (in the flesh), you have to go back, make things right, and start all over again. It's called rebuilding the foundation.

Look at the Tower of Babel. In Genesis 11:4 we read,

And they said, "Come, let us build ourselves a city, and

a tower whose top is in the heavens; let us make a name for ourselves, lest we be scattered abroad over the face of the whole earth."

This city and tower were constructed in order to build a name for man, not God. Its very purpose and dedication was again, "flesh." In Romans 7:18 Paul states,

For I know that in me [that is, in my flesh] nothing good dwells; for to will is present with me, but how to perform what is good I do not find.

The flesh cannot understand the plans of the Father, obey them or fulfill them. God cannot, and will not, use anything that is flesh-born or motivated. The flesh brings no positive spiritual return, which the raven in its non-stop flight from the ark illustrates. As I mentioned earlier, this bird was driven by its appetite for more dead flesh, not a quest for dry land.

Noah and his family were seeking to know how much longer it would be until they would depart from the ark. This was a spiritual question in response to an action God initiated when He closed the door to the ark. Since it was God who shut the ark's door, it would have to be God who would open it as well. Scripture teaches when God closes a door no one can open it. In this same way, when He opens a door, no one can shut it. Revelation 3:7 says,

These things says He who is holy, He who is true, He who has the key of David, He who opens and no one shuts, and shuts and no one opens.

Through the raven, God was illustrating to us that when

His Spirit leads us into a situation, it will also have to be His Spirit that leads us out. What begins in the Spirit must always finish in the Spirit, not in the flesh.

Abraham and Sarah learned this lesson. In Genesis 15:1-4, God promised them that they would give birth to a son who would become their sole heir. When they first heard this word, there was great rejoicing, but as is with many of God's promises, there was a great span of time in between the promise and its fulfillment. Because of a lack of patience on Sarah's part, she implemented her own plan in an effort to bring the promise to fruition as found in Genesis 16:1-4. She convinced Abraham and her handmaiden Hagar to have sexual relations in hopes that this would fulfill the promise God had given Abraham. Well, it didn't! In fact, as we have seen, it had exactly the opposite effect. What begins in the Spirit must always finish in the Spirit. The only thing Sarah's plan produced was more flesh. The son Abraham and Hagar produced was named Ishmael who later became the father of the Arab nations, and now the aftermath of this impatient act is being felt even unto this day. What begins in the Spirit must always finish in the Spirit.

This same principle applies to the end-time revival that is about to be poured out from heaven. God's plan was set in motion 2000 years ago when Mary conceived the Messiah within her womb. What began in the Spirit then will eventually, in His time, finish in the Spirit. This revival will have nothing to do with the resources of man. It won't be built around a big name, nor will it require a big facility with a big choir. It will not be reserved for those who are able to underwrite a big event with their big budget. No, this revival will come to those who have a big heart for their big God! Don't get me wrong, I'm not against big things. Look at the ark, it wasn't little, it was huge, but the key wasn't its size, but rather the Father's purpose behind it.

The ark didn't give birth to the flood, the flood gave birth to the ark. If there had been no flood, there wouldn't have been any need for the ark. So many times we get the cart before the horse. We wind up looking at the effect instead of the cause. It's Holy Ghost revival that causes an unknown preacher to become a well-known preacher overnight. It's revival that gives birth to nightly church meetings packed to capacity. It's revival that pays off the existing church mortgage and raises the money in full for the new sanctuary. Remember, the ark didn't give birth to the flood, the flood gave birth to the ark. And this same principle applies to revival. Once the tactics and energies of the flesh are removed from our lives and ministries, then the Father has the freedom to release from heaven the blessings He has prepared.

The Three Sendings

Following the fruitless effort of the raven, Noah released a dove from the window to see whether or not their departure from the ark was drawing near. This was a very significant action taken by the man of God, because prophetically there is a powerful message behind this event. Genesis 8:8-12 reads,

> *He also sent out from himself a dove, to see if the waters had receded from the face of the ground. But the dove found no resting place for the sole of her foot, and she returned into the ark to him, for the waters were on the face of the whole earth. So he put out his hand and took her, and drew her into the ark to himself. And he waited yet another seven days, and again he sent the dove out from the ark. Then the dove came to him in the evening, and behold a freshly plucked olive leaf was*

*in her mouth; and Noah knew that the waters had re-
ceded from the earth. So he waited yet another seven
days and sent out the dove, which did not return again
to him anymore.*

I believe these three sendings of the dove are a typology
illustrating three distinct divine revelations God would send
from heaven to earth. With each sending would come a personal revelation, focusing separately on each person of the
Godhead, beginning with God the Son, continuing with
God the Holy Spirit, and then climaxing with God the
Father.

Remember, earlier on in our studies, we saw that Noah
is a type of God the Father. We also examined how the ark is
likened unto a "mini-earth," which was never intended by
God to be a permanent dwelling place. Even when man was
created and placed in the Garden, it was never God's intent
that we be separated from Him. From the book of Genesis
to Malachi, you will find that the Old Testament revelation
of God was the forerunner sent in order to prepare the way
for each of these divine revelations.

In Galatians 3:24-25, Paul calls the law his tutor or
schoolteacher.

*Therefore the law was our tutor to bring us to Christ,
that we might be justified by faith. But after faith has
come, we are no longer under a tutor.*

The ministry of John the Baptist illustrates this as well.
Matthew 3:3 reads,

*For this is he who was spoken of by the prophet Isaiah,
saying: "The voice of one crying in the wilderness:
Prepare the way of the Lord; Make His paths straight."*

Just as John the Baptist, the last of the Old Testament prophets, was the forerunner for Jesus, the law was the forerunner for the intimacy we would enjoy with God under the new covenant of grace.

After the groundwork had been laid under the old covenant, the world was now ready for this threefold revelation of God. It was always God's intention for man to know Him in His fullness and to fully abide in His presence. Jesus said in John 14:2,

> *In My Father's house are many mansions; if it were not so, I would have told you. I go to prepare a place for you.*

The Father wants us with Him and the first step towards getting us there was by sending His Son, the first dove.

The First Dove

In Genesis 8:8-9 we read,

> *He also sent out from himself a dove, to see if the waters had receded from the face of the ground. But the dove found no resting place for the sole of her foot, and she returned into the ark to him, for the waters were on the face of the whole earth. So he put out his hand and took her, and drew her into the ark to himself.*

As we consider the symbolism associated with this historical event, I believe when Noah released the dove for the first time from the ark, that this was representative of God the Father sending His only Son from heaven to earth. Jesus was sinless, but yet He became sin for the entire human race so that we might walk in relationship and fellowship with

God. If man was going to experience friendship with God, then his sins had to be dealt with, and this is what Jesus made possible. Paul puts it this way in 2 Corinthians 5:21,

> *For He made Him who knew no sin to be sin for us, that we might become the righteousness of God in Him.*

There are no shortcuts to the Father. It all begins with Jesus. If we are going to know God the way He desires for us to know Him, then we need to embrace the One who was sent in His likeness. You can't love the Father and reject His Son. If someone genuinely loves me, they will also love my children. My personality, physical abilities, academic strengths, and other talents and gifts have been genetically placed within them. Many times I have heard people remark regarding my children, "They are just like Craig." Or they may say, "That is definitely their father speaking." In some respects, when you have seen my kids, you have seen me.

As we have seen, Philip, one of Jesus' disciples, wanted to see God the Father. He knew Jesus had an earthly father, but all of this talk about God the Father was foreign to Philip. In order to resolve his questions, he asks Jesus to physically introduce the Father to him and he'll be settled about the entire issue. Look again at the response of Jesus in John 14:9.

> *Jesus said to him, "Have I been with you so long, and yet you have not known Me, Philip? He who has seen Me has seen the Father; so how can you say, 'Show us the Father.'"*

No one will ever experience relationship and fellowship with the Father unless they come through His Son Jesus first.

Once an individual experiences salvation, this is only the beginning of their spiritual journey, not the end. Salvation is the first step towards knowing the Father. Once that step has been taken, we are ready for the next divine revelation, the second dove.

The Second Dove

After the dove was released the first time, scripture records it returned to Noah because there was no dry ground to be found. Then after a seven-day waiting period, he released the dove a second time. Genesis 8:10-11 states,

And he waited yet another seven days, and again he sent the dove out from the ark. Then the dove came to him in the evening, and behold, a freshly plucked olive leaf was in her mouth; and Noah knew that the waters had receded from the earth.

This second sending is another powerful prophetic promise. This time when the dove returned, it had an olive leaf in its mouth. The major difference between the first and the second sending is the olive leaf. God was illustrating to us that the second visitation would center around a revelation of the Holy Spirit. In the Scriptures, olive oil almost always refers to the Holy Spirit, such as when Samuel went to the house of Jesse to anoint a new King over Israel. First Samuel 16:12-13 records,

So he sent and brought him in. Now he was ruddy, with bright eyes, and good-looking. And the Lord said, "Arise, anoint him; for this is the one." Then Samuel took the horn of oil and anointed him in the midst of

his brothers; and the Spirit of the Lord came upon David from that day forward. So Samuel arose and went to Ramah.

When he saw David, he prophesied and then poured olive oil over David's head. The poured oil represented the Holy Spirit anointing David with the authority to occupy the throne as Israel's next king.

Another example is found in John 12:1-8 when Mary the sister of Martha washed the feet of Jesus and anointed Him with costly olive oil that had been fragranced with spikenard. When Judas challenged the action as an extravagant waste of money, Jesus brought correction on him by stating in verse 7, "Leave her alone; she has kept this for the day of My burial." Her action was an outward demonstration of the Holy Spirit anointing Jesus with the authority and strength to lay His life down for the sins of the world.

When the dove returned after her second sending with an olive leaf in her mouth, God was showing us that man would experience the power of the Holy Spirit in ways known only to God prior to the cross. Because of what Jesus accomplished, the moment we experience salvation, the same anointing and authority that Jesus walked in during His earthly ministry is now available to us. The Holy Spirit lived in Jesus, and because of our salvation experience, He now lives in us. Jesus knew the voice and leading of the Holy Spirit and now every Christian has this benefit available as well. Scripture declares we are now joint heirs with Jesus. That means His spiritual inheritance is also ours. The bottom line is, we now have access to a dimension in the Holy Spirit that was never available before the Cross.

In earlier reading about the different moves of God throughout history, didn't you find it amazing that since the

Day of Pentecost every revival has emphasized either Jesus or the Holy Spirit? For the first two millennia since the resurrection of Jesus Christ, every major move of God has centered around a revelation of either God the Son or God the Holy Spirit. Not once has there been a movement emphasizing God the Father. That's where the symbol of Noah sending the dove the third time comes into play.

The Third Dove

In Genesis 8:12 we read,

So he waited yet another seven days and sent out the dove, which did not return again to him anymore.

This is a powerful scripture when it comes to eschatology. We have just examined two sendings and now a third sending has taken place and it's over. Here is Noah, a type of God the Father, releasing a dove three times, which I believe represents three distinct divine revelations. After the dove's third release, we see that it never returns again because this symbolizes the final revelation God has reserved for mankind—a revelation of the Father Himself.

The Father is about to reveal Himself, in a way the world has never experienced before, in what I believe God has called "The Greatest Awakening." All of the pain from unholy father figures will be healed at that time. The distrust, bitterness, and emptiness people have been living with from generation to generation will be supernaturally removed from their hearts. The fatherless will find in God the Father what they always longed for. Men and women who thought they could never be made whole will be wondrously transformed by this holy wave.

133

Second Wave

When the Father originally gave me the vision of two waves, the second wave I saw was greater in power and strength than the first. This wave will cause all walls of opposition to crumble worldwide. Religious strongholds, which have held nations in their demonic grip, will lose their hold when this outpouring of the Father is released. The second wave I saw coming will take away everything that is not of God in its path. There is no stopping it. The Lord has decreed it!

There have been two millennia since the life of Christ. It's almost as if God had dedicated one thousand years towards knowing His Son and an additional thousand years towards knowing His Holy Spirit. What's left? Matthew 24:37 teaches that before the Lord returns it will be just like it was in the days of Noah. Here we are now just entering into the third millennium. Scripture teaches in 2 Peter 3:8,

> *But beloved, do not forget this one thing, that with the Lord one day is as a thousand years, and a thousand years as one day.*

Wasn't Jonah in the belly of a large fish for three days and nights before his release? Wasn't Jesus in the belly of the earth for three days and nights prior to His resurrection? We have entered into the third day or third millennium. This is the Father's millennium and He is about to reveal Himself to the world in a way that has never been experienced in all of church history.

After this great move, just as Noah, his family, and the animal life departed from the temporary dwelling of the ark, the Church is going to depart from this temporary dwelling

134

called earth to another dwelling place called the Kingdom of heaven.

Fire Starter

Since the Lord has placed this mantle on me, my personal life and ministry have not been the same. I shared with you how God came to me in Brazil and placed something in my hand. It wasn't until I was in Perth, Australia, two years later that the Lord revealed to me exactly what He put there. I had just finished a week-long crusade that proved to be spiritually very fruitful. People were saying goodbye to one another, and it was at this point an old Welshman who had been attending the meetings approached me and said, "Pastor, would you allow us, as leaders, to pray for you?" I was blessed by the invitation and graciously agreed. When he began to pray, heaven came down and he began to prophesy and the word of the Lord astounded me. By the Holy Spirit's anointing, he began to recount perfectly what had happened to me in Brazil, including the dates and times, with precise accuracy.

Please read the word for yourselves. "Two years ago you were in a foreign country and during your stay there, I came to you with a special impartation. I told you before you went that you would be a carrier. I told you I would come and place something in your hand. I also said that you would carry what I put there to the nations. For two years you have asked me what it was I placed in your hand. Some tried to tell you what it was, but they were wrong. Tonight I'm going to tell you Myself. I have placed a supernatural fire in your hand. Yes, you are a fire starter in the Spirit. You will go to places people have called impossible, and it will be easy. To prove to you that I am speaking, your hands will begin to burn with holy fire right now."

When the Lord said "now," I was knocked to the floor and remained there for at least two hours.

We are in the final stages of history as we know it. The Lord's return is closer than ever. There is a revival coming that is beyond words and the Holy Spirit is calling you to be part of it. He wants you to be a fire starter too. There is an impartation waiting for you, an impartation of the Father's heart. Allow the Holy Spirit to prepare you for this awakening, yes, this "Greatest Awakening" that will bring in the final harvest. Then after this, 1 Thessalonians 4: 16-17 will be fulfilled.

For the Lord Himself will descend from heaven with a shout, with the voice of an archangel, and with the trumpet of God, And the dead in Christ will rise first. Then we who are alive and remain shall be caught up together with them in the clouds to meet the Lord in the air. And thus we shall always be with the Lord (NKJV).

CLOSING PRAYER

This book has been about a journey; a journey that changed my life and which, I trust, has impacted yours. If I leave you at this point, all I have left you with is a good story. You don't need another story; you need to experience the truth you've just read about. Spiritually, you are now standing at the door of entrance into the Father's heart. Let me encourage you to take the next step. Step through the door and into the presence of the Father. In His presence, there is healing for broken hearts and minds. In His presence, we exchange our sorrow for His joy. In His presence, we trade our weakness for His strength. In His presence, we lay down our failures and embrace His victory. Yes, in His presence, we are eternally transformed.

This transformation can't be bought and sold. It can only be revealed and received. Revealed by the Holy Spirit and, like our salvation experience, received with a willing heart. Are you ready? Are you willing? The Father is. In fact, this divine appointment was established for your life even before the sands of time. He wants to be the Father for whom you have always longed. Look at the Father's fruit. The life of Jesus is a testimony of His faithfulness.

My words to you are, "Let the testimony begin." From this day forward, your life will never be the same. Get ready to receive the Father's Heart. In preparation for this moment, please find a quiet place with privacy and pray this prayer.

Father, in Jesus' name I come to You just as I am. I desire more! I want all that You have prepared for me. I want to know You as Jesus knows You. I desire to walk with You as Jesus walks with You. I want to be one with You and know You as the faithful loving Father that You are. I renounce every hindrance, I renounce every sin, I renounce every stronghold that would stand between You and me. Baptize me with Your heart. Fill me with Your love. Like David, make me a person after Your own heart. I thank you in Jesus' name that You've heard and answered my prayer. Amen!

Now begin to thank the Father for answering your prayer. Many of you may feel something welling up within your heart. That's the Holy Spirit piercing you with the Father's heart. Don't be afraid of what is happening. Yield to it. Cry out for more. This is only the beginning. Moment by moment, day-by-day, and week-by-week, this intimacy will continue to grow and grow and grow. There's no end to His presence because there is no end to Him. Just keep receiving all the Father has for you.

The day the Father touched me in this way, I felt like my heart was being filled up like a hot water bottle. This experience was so overwhelming that I thought my heart was going to explode. The truth is, the Father was enlarging my heart and increasing my capacity to love and be loved because He is love!

Now He has begun this process in you. Your heart is going through a transformation. You will never be the same. The way you view yourself is about to change. The way you view others is about to change. You're looking through different eyes now. You're looking through the eyes of the

Father. He sees what people do not see. He sees the final product. So, don't run *from* His arms, run *into* His arms. This is not a onetime encounter, but an ongoing revelation. We are a work in progress going from glory to glory. During His earthly walk, Jesus was the exact replica of the Father and now, through us, the Father continues to reveal Himself to a lost and hurting world.

About the Author

As a gifted speaker and author with more than twenty years of pastoral experience, Craig Lauterbach travels throughout the United States and internationally sharing a balanced message of faith and inspiration.

Many have referred to Craig as a "Bridge Builder" in the Body of Christ, thus opening doors to minister with people such as Tommy Barnett, Dr. David Yonggi Cho, Jesse Duplantis, and even former Vice President Dan Quayle. He is an honorary board member of the Los Angeles International Church (Dream Center) in California, which also recognizes Jack Hayford, E.V. Hill, Charles Nieman, Willie George, and Jack Wallace as members.

Together with his wife Cindy, he carries the message of the Father's heart to a lost and hurting world.

Contact the author for speaking engagements
at the address below:

CRAIG LAUTERBACH MINISTRIES
P.O. BOX 201
PIPERSVILLE, PA 18947 USA
(215) 766-7007 • FAX (215) 766-8676
e-mail: CLMIN@verizon.net

C.L.M.
TAPE RESOURCE LIBRARY

SPIRITUAL GIFTS & MINISTRIES (#0777)
(Audio cassette 9-tape series) - $40.00 (US)
This teaching series is an in-depth study on the nine super-natural gifts of the Holy Spirit and explains their manifestation and operation in relation to the five-fold and seven-fold offices of the church. This study will help you discover the ministry God has called you to as a disciple and provide Biblical guidance for orderly flow in the gifts of the Spirit.

THE WARRIOR SPIRIT (#0778)
(Audio cassette 8-tape series) - $35.00 (US)
Many Christians are living their lives on the defensive rather than on the offensive. The Father has not called us to have a survivor spirit, but to take on the spirit of a WARRIOR. Find out why you are the greatest nightmare the Devil has to face. This series on the warrior spirit will help the listener understand the weapons they have been equipped with and how to utilize them. If you're tired of living in defeat, this study is for you!

THE ARMOR OF GOD (#0779)
(Audio cassette 8-tape series) - $35.00 (US)
There has been much confusion regarding the "Armor Of God." On one end, people have neglected the armor and found themselves in spiritual warfare without any protection. Then on the other end, people have entered into mysticism allowing the armor to become a superstitious act. God the Father wants believers to understand the weapons they have been given for establishing His kingdom on earth.

Putting on the full armor of God is not a physical act, but a spiritual mindset. This study will open your eyes, strengthen your faith and usher you higher to a new level of effectiveness in your ministry and daily life.

THE MANTLE OF INTERCESSION (#0780)
(Audio cassette 6-tape series) - $25.00 (US)
Intercession is the foundation on which our spiritual growth and ministries are built. Jesus was a man of prayer! Prior to every significant event in His life, you will find Him alone with the Father. If the Son of God depended on the dynamo of prayer for success, then how much more us? This series will challenge, equip, and transform the listener's prayer life into one of intimacy and power.

CALLED TO BE FREE (#0781)
(Audio cassette 5-tape series) - $20.00 (US)
The Father has ordained that we experience the fullness of our inheritance as sons and daughters. God has declared that we should be blessed in the City and blessed in the field. Jesus stated that He came that we might have abundant life. If the blessing and abundance is lacking in our lives, we need to make sure there are no issues in the heart hindering us from receiving His abundance. This series will help us recognize and remove the spiritual road blocks keeping us from His blessing.

THE KINGDOM OF GOD (#0782)
(Audio cassette 5-tape series) - $20.00 (US)
There is a purpose and flow of authority that Jesus walked in that must be manifest in the Body of Christ if genuine revival is to be released. This teaching series reveals how Jesus came to do the will of the Father, Jesus came to speak the

words of the Father and Jesus came to glorify the Father. If we are going to experience the fullness of the anointing Jesus walked in, then we must embrace His same passion for the Father.

To Place an Order

When purchasing product from the C.L.M. Tape Resource Library, all checks or money orders should be made payable to: "Craig Lauterbach Ministries, C.L.M." There is an additional $4.00 shipping and handling charge for each item purchased. When ordering bulk quantities of these tapes, please contact the C.L.M. office for special pricing and shipping arrangements.

C.L.M.
P.O. Box 201
Pipersville, Pennsylvania, 18947
(215) 766-7007